PARENTING MY FATHER

A JOURNEY WITH DEMENTIA

by

Claire Virginia McCulloch

authorHOUSE®

AuthorHouse™
1663 Liberty Drive, Suite 200
Bloomington, IN 47403
www.authorhouse.com
Phone: 1-800-839-8640

First published by AuthorHouse 3/21/2008

ISBN: 978-1-4343-6386-2 (sc)

Library of Congress Control Number: 2008900761

Printed in the United States of America
Bloomington, Indiana

This book is printed on acid-free paper.

For all who helped me on this journey,
with love and gratitude.

CHAPTER 1

MY FATHER'S LIFE ENDS

JANUARY 9, 2003, CRANFORD, NEW JERSEY

Dad was ninety-two when he died in his house, in the town he called home for some sixty years. His actual death wasn't much of a struggle, for which we are all thankful. For months he had been slowly failing, both physically and mentally. The week before he died, I noticed that when he wasn't sleeping, he was quite still in bed, staring upwards. He seemed so calm and peaceful, as if his soul was in transition between earth and Heaven. That final day, Annette, Dad's live-in home health aide, called the Hospice nurse to report that his breathing became labored, so oxygen was brought in and administered. Dad's last conscious act before he died was to pull the tube away from his nose, clearly indicating his wishes. By the time I got to his house, his breathing had stopped, but his heart was still weakly fluttering. I cradled his skinny, still-warm body in my arms and held fast, although I knew he was slipping away. Sobbing, I wished him a good journey towards Heaven to meet Mom and others who were already there waiting. I mentioned each family member here on earth and told him we would be fine with him keeping watch over us. The Hospice nurse then took over for the official pronouncement of death, and Annette and I had a good cry. As well prepared as I thought I was for this day, my heart ached with the reality of his passing. How I would miss this special man!

The story I want to share chronicles my father's life before his dementia, as well as my involvement near the end, when I witnessed first-hand the slow deterioration of a once beautiful mind. I know Dad would not want this book to be overly sad, so I will relate many of the uplifting moments and focus on the times we laughed over his eccentricities.

As our population ages, much attention is given to Alzheimer's disease, which is the most common form of dementia. President Reagan's long struggle was heart-wrenching for his family, particularly when he lost the ability to communicate or recognize them. My father, however, was able to recite his own full name two weeks before he died, so I was not convinced when I read on his certificate that the cause of death was Alzheimer's.

In the final analysis, it doesn't really matter what form of dementia he had. The important focus is the life Millard Obrig Hallenbeck led and the legacy he left behind. In his last few years, our roles slowly reversed. As he became more forgetful and child-like, I found myself acting in a more protective and nurturing way, like a parent guiding a child. There were times during this journey when I felt incredibly sad and overwhelmed with the responsibility, but Mil's happy spirit and silliness often lifted my mood and put joy into my heart. I became drawn into his world of living in the present and learned to appreciate life in a newly profound way.

To tell this story honors my father and helps keep his memory alive for all of us who have been touched by his spirit.

Chapter 2

My Father's Life Begins

September 22, 1910, Brooklyn, New York

My father was an only child, yet I never heard him say that he was lonely growing up or that he wished he had siblings. He was doted on by his grandparents, aunts and uncles, and he had many friends and cousins for playmates. His baby book is a treasure, filled with wonderful photographs and descriptions of his growth and development. His mother, Anna Obrig Hallenbeck, was our family historian. I discovered my grandmother's genealogy notebooks in Dad's house and spent countless hours reading about our ancestors.

Nana, as we called her, was descended from the Herzogs, owners of several wineries in Switzerland. Nana's maternal grandparents, Anna and Joseph Herzog, emigrated to America in 1852 with their twelve younger children. Their plan was to reunite with their two eldest daughters who had settled earlier in New York with their husbands. Tragically, a typhoid epidemic broke out on their ship and took the life of Joseph, who was buried at sea. His wife also became ill, and while she was recovering in a New York hospital, her twelve younger children were divided up and taken in by their older sisters. I can only imagine how traumatized they were by these events. Fortunately, Anna

3

Herzog not only recovered, but she lived a long time and had numerous grandchildren. Her namesake eventually became my father's mother. Although Nana was only five when her grandmother died, she lovingly remembered her singing German lullabies.

The Obrigs, on the paternal side of Nana's family, date back to 1756 in Wermelskirchen, Germany. Her grandfather, Gerhard Jacob Obrig, was born in 1815; he married Meta Newburg, and eventually they moved to Brooklyn, New York. There they bought a large house and raised ten children, including Ernst Obrig, Nana's father. He married Lena Herzog in 1865 when they were just teenagers. They looked so young in their wedding picture I thought they resembled children playing dress-up in their parents' clothing. That photograph was printed onto an invitation to their lavish fiftieth anniversary celebration at the Bossert Hotel in Brooklyn in 1915. Ernst lived to be eighty-one and Lena seventy-eight. Other than an occasional infant or child mortality, many Obrig ancestors lived into their eighties and beyond.

Nana was born on January 30, 1880, and she was named Anna Franziska Obrig. As the youngest of seven, she was given much attention from her older siblings. One of her earliest memories was of her Grandpa Obrig dressing up in a santa suit for Saint Nicholas Day, celebrated by Germans on December 6. Nana and her cousins would bang on pots and pans as Santa threw candies from his bag. The older boys would knock over the pots and pans and grab candy from the little ones, making them cry. As grandmothers do, Grandma Obrig restored peace in the family by serving milk and cookies.

Anna Obrig graduated in 1900 with a teaching degree from Normal College in New York, which later became Hunter College. She taught elementary school briefly and performed ballet in a dance troupe called the Flora Dora Girls. An older sister took her on a European tour, and Nana's diary recorded their adventures. Shipboard activities included performing skits for the captain in the evening. I doubt that few young ladies in the early 1900's led as privileged and exciting a life as my grandmother.

When Nana married Millard Fillmore Hallenbeck, Jr. in 1909, she was three months shy of her thirtieth birthday. Soon she began researching her husband's family tree. Abraham Hallenbeck married Jane Van Hoesen in 1830 when they were teenagers. They emigrated from Holland to settle in the Catskill Mountains, New York. The last of their seven children was born in 1850 and named after President Millard Fillmore, whom they supported. Millard F. Hallenbeck married Mary Chambers in 1877. Four of Mary's eight siblings had died in childhood, and she was the only one to marry. Mary and Millard had their first child in 1879 and named him Millard Fillmore Hallenbeck, Jr. They then had two daughters, one of whom died at the age of two. The other, Edythe, married and had one child in 1918 named Robert Wilcox, who is Dad's only cousin on his father's side. Although Edythe died in her forties, Dr. Wilcox is an active theologian in Tennessee. Mary Chambers Hallenbeck died at the age of seventy-nine and her husband at age eighty-one. Their son, who became Dad's father, lived to be eighty-two.

How I would have loved to discuss Nana's genealogy notes with my father! Sadly, by the time I located the notebooks, Dad had serious memory problems and was unable to comprehend the significance of family history. In contrast, his mother's mind remained sharp until she died in 1978 at the age of ninety-eight. My family is eternally grateful to Nana for the gift she left us. Her meticulously detailed records help keep the past alive.

CHAPTER 3

MILLARD GROWS UP

Millard Obrig Hallenbeck, beloved only child of Anna and Millard, grew up in Brooklyn, New York. To escape the city heat in summer, he vacationed with relatives in Brielle at the Jersey shore, in Patchogue, Long Island, and at various lakes and farms in upstate New York. One of my discoveries in Dad's attic was a shoebox filled with fading photos of my father playing with his Obrig cousins. In a letter written to his grandparents in 1923, young Millard described riding a "twenty-three year old pony that was still frisky," swimming in a cold river, and eating "three frankfurters fried on a campfire." It seems that this city boy had plenty of adventures in the country. He was always tall for his age as he grew up, and his hair stayed blonde until his early teens.

My grandfather worked for an insurance company until he was well into his seventies. Nana played bridge, entertained frequently, and taught Sunday School at the Ocean Avenue Congregational Church where my father sang in the youth choir.

While in elementary school, Dad was permitted to skip a grade, so that when he entered James Madison High School, he was not quite thirteen. A high percentage of his graduating class went on to college.

When Dad began his freshman year at Dartmouth College in 1927, he was not yet seventeen. It had been very difficult to get a spot in that freshman class. Although more that 2,200 men had applied for 626 spaces, only 35 percent were accepted. Dad's parents were reluctant to have their only child travel so far from home to attend college, but they changed their minds when the minister's son, George Miller, was also accepted.

My father wrote home that he slept very little on the long train ride to New Hampshire, because he looked out the window at every stop along the way. Nana saved all of her son's correspondence from 1927 – 1931, giving our family wonderful insight into Mil's college life.

Traditionally, Dartmouth sophomores were expected to initiate hazing rituals for the freshmen. When Dad was ordered to sing a Prohibition-era lyric *How Dry I Am*, he was soon drenched with a bucketful of water! Punishment for disobeying a request from an upperclassman resulted in a whack on the backside with a wooden paddle.

My father auditioned and was accepted into the Glee Club, and he joined the Outing Club so that he could explore the White Mountains. He wrote about disappointing his father, who had hoped he would try out for the swim team. Dad declined because he was underweight for his tall frame and fearful of the exertion. He and his buddies attended movies in town where they would throw peanuts and shout at the villains on the screen. Packages containing sweets and snacks from his mother and aunts were welcomed, and Dad was always writing home for more money. Prohibition did not stop a bootlegger from operating on campus between stints in the local jail. Smoking was allowed even in the classroom, and one of Dad's professors passed out cigarettes to the students. Apparently even the physical education teachers believed that there was no harm in having a cigarette or two after a meal as long as you did not smoke excessively on an empty stomach! Dad wrote home that he had not *yet* given in to the temptation.

Although my father scored well on a freshman intelligence test, he worried about his grades and his perpetual slowness, a trait that lasted his entire life. He confessed that often he was the last in class to finish an exam and the last to finish eating in the cafeteria. Dad always took a long time with his meals, and when he was an old man with dementia, his slowness became even more pronounced.

One of the worst natural disasters in New England history was a devastating flood in early November, 1927. Torrential rain and melting snow caused the Connecticut River to swell thirty feet above its normal level. My father was one of about a thousand Dartmouth students recruited by the Red Cross to help clear debris around White River Junction. After traveling in an unheated boxcar in twenty-six degree weather, these young men worked knee-deep in mud all day long. With his usual wit, Dad wrote home: "If there were any more floods, surely I would qualify for a D.D. degree – *Ditch Digger*." At the end of his life, even when he remembered little else, he never forgot his years at Dartmouth.

Some of my father's classmates had to leave college in their senior year due to financial hardship caused by the Great Depression. It must have been a strain for my grandfather as well, since he worked strictly on commission at Traveler's Insurance Company. In spite of Dad's scholastic worries, he qualified for the honor society Phi Beta Kappa and graduated Cum Laude on June 16, 1931. There were 432 men in his graduating class, nearly 200 less than in his freshman year. With a major in English, Mil hoped to start a career in business.

Times were hard and jobs were scarce. Dad moved back in with his parents in Brooklyn who supported him while he searched for work. Finally an uncle got him a job showing toys made by a blind man to retail stores. He wore out the soles of his shoes going door-to-door, but he was grateful for the ten dollars a week salary. His next job was in the collections department of the Brooklyn Union Gas Company. One of his responsibilities was to dispatch men to the homes of delinquent bill payers in order to shut off their gas supply. My father stayed at this job for five years, ending with a salary of twenty-six dollars a week.

During his bachelor years, Dad re-connected with his childhood friend Claude Grady and maintained a friendship with George Miller and other college men. He kept meticulous records of football games as he listened to them on the radio. Although Mil had a few dates in college, the special girl who caught his attention was right there in the Flatbush section of Brooklyn. Her name was Marion Henrietta Newton.

CHAPTER 4

FAMILY MAN

My parents met at the Ocean Avenue Congregational Church in Brooklyn, where both of their families had been active for years. In December 1937 they announced their engagement. My mother worked as a secretary in The Brooklyn Trust Company, and my father commuted to his new job in Kearny, New Jersey. He started at Western Electric Company as a Merchandise Estimator and worked his way up to Section Chief in the Personnel Department. His employment record states that upon hire he was six feet two inches tall and only 160 pounds! He had a high forehead with a receding hairline, and he wore wire-rimmed glasses which made him look quite intellectual. Mom was small-framed and a foot shorter than her handsome beau, but she often wore very high heels.

Marion and Mil were married on April 21, 1939, by Reverend George Miller, Sr. They left Brooklyn and settled in a tiny apartment in Belleville, New Jersey, to be closer to Dad's job. After their baby Lois Ann was born in 1941, they moved to a two-family house in Belleville. Next they re-located to a bungalow on Hillcrest Avenue in Cranford, and I came along in 1945.

It was fun growing up in that neighborhood, where the houses were close together and there were lots of kids my age for playmates. Mom drove Dad to the train station each morning so that she could take her daughters to our activities. She was our emotional disciplinarian and Dad was the quiet provider. I loved snuggling in his lap to hear him sing his Dartmouth songs or listen to him read the *funnies* from the Sunday paper. I remember feeling safe and secure in his long arms.

My mother became dissatisfied with our little house, and she persuaded Dad to buy a bigger one in a new development across town. When we moved to Brookdale Road in the fall of 1956, I felt as though I was worlds away from my old neighborhood. I even missed the sidewalks and curbs. I found out years later that it really strapped Dad financially to move at that time. Still, he managed to pay off his mortgage in ten years.

Lois married Cranford native Bill Roesel in 1961, and over time they had four children. By that time Dad was a Military Contract Buyer at Bell Laboratories. He handled difficult contract negotiations with officials from the U.S. Army Anti-Ballistic Missile Safeguard Program. His career with the Bell System spanned thirty-eight years. At his retirement luncheon in 1975, he was given notes of appreciation from his colleagues for his professionalism and respectful manner.

Although my parents loved to travel, they were happiest when caring for their grandchildren. John McCulloch and I married in 1970 and gave them two more. All six loved taking turns staying at Grandma and Papa's house. A permanent playroom was set up on the fourth floor of their split-level home, where toys could be left out until the next visit. The doting grandparents found time to become involved in all of the kids' activities and took them on vacations and to zoos and museums. My nephew Steven referred to them as his *fun parents*.

My father was the last grandparent to die. After his funeral, his adult grandchildren, who had flown in from all over the country and even abroad, gathered in Papa's *rec room* to swap stories. Laughter and silliness prevailed as they shared memories about growing up with such energetic grandparents. They blew bubbles and tried on Papa's hats. At one point I heard shrieks as my nephew David tried to lift my daughter Kristen up into the laundry chute. It was the last time we would all be together in that house. A chapter was closing in our lives, but the memories would last forever.

CHAPTER 5

WARNING SIGNS

Now that some time has passed since my father's death, I can look back and review the early signs that something was wrong. I try to recall when it all began and think about any steps that could have been taken earlier to prevent or delay the symptoms of dementia.

Dad was devastated when Mom died at age seventy-four on January 12, 1990, after suffering a stroke on New Year's Eve. Our parents had celebrated their fiftieth wedding anniversary the previous April. Without his wife, it seemed at first that Dad would be lost. Most of our family was still in New Jersey at the time of her death. Lois became Dad's date for senior events and encouraged him to hire a cleaning lady. Soon his friends got him involved in playing mixed bridge and picked him up on Saturday mornings for breakfast. He attended Old Guard meetings for retired businessmen. His church urged him to join the choir and welcomed his rich bass voice. He helped deliver meals to shut-ins and joined a group of men who took turns locking up the church at night. Always an avid reader, he kept his mind active by doing crossword puzzles, reading newspapers and magazines. He had regular physical exams, took vitamins, gave up smoking, and had a healthy appetite. He exercised regularly by taking his poodle Randi on long walks and runs in the park. After Marion's death, the dog formed a strong bond with Mil and gave him a reason to get up each day.

Dad loved swimming! His stroke was unusual: one arm gave a quick pull in the water while the other very slowly reached high into the air as he nearly flipped over onto his back. His stamina lasted well into his eighties, when he would swim twenty laps at a time at the Cranford Swim Club, which he helped organize back in the 1950's. As a little girl I can remember his excitement when he showed me the plans for this pool. His name is still on a commemorative plaque over the drinking fountain at the site.

Ocean swimming was pleasurable for Dad as well. I remember anxiously watching his bald head as he slowly swam far out in the waves at Ortley Beach when he visited us at our summer house. He would finally emerge from the surf shivering but grinning all over, just like a little kid. It would bring back childhood memories when he would take us swimming in Paulins Kill Lake or Estling Lake or in the ocean at Asbury Park. I was never afraid in the water because of the protection of my father's long arms. As he became frail with age, I felt as though he needed *me* to try and keep *him* safe!

My sister and her husband had him up to their summer house in the Pocono Mountains in Pennsylvania, where he was able to exhibit his swimming skills and soak up the country air. Dad seemed to have recovered from Mom's death with the help of family and friends, and he appeared to be quite happy and healthy.

Lois and Bill retired to North Carolina in 1997. Eventually all four of their children, Gary, David, Steven, and Bonnie moved to other states. Our two children, Johnny and Kristen, were still in New Jersey but were busy with their jobs and studies.

Mil was busy with numerous activities, many of which included his lady friend Alice. I think during this time he saw more of her than us, but we were willing to give him space because he was so happy.

Gradually Dad seemed to be getting more and more forgetful. I decided to drive over one Saturday in February, 1999, and give him a memory test as part of a homework assignment I had from college. The test is called *The Mini-Mental State Exam* and consists of simple questions, calculations, writing, and copying a design. Dad scored well, getting twenty-eight correct answers out of thirty. I figured that if he could count backwards by sevens and knew the President's name as well as the correct date, I didn't have to worry. After all, Dad was nothing like the confused patients I frequently saw in my job as nursing supervisor for Bayada Nurses, a home care agency.

His intellect prevailed, but Dad's forgetfulness escalated to periods of confusion. He was clever enough to recognize that something was wrong and to hide it from his family. After living for fifty years with a wife who worried about everything, Dad certainly did not want his daughters interfering with his newly independent life! He always told us that everything was all right, and we believed him.

Memory problems associated with dementia are often insidious, and part of the problem is that families are either in denial or just don't know what to do. It wasn't until I got a troubling phone call in late spring of 1999 that I realized the seriousness of Dad's mental condition.

CHAPTER 6

BLESS FRAN!

The older I get the more I am convinced that God sends someone into our lives at the right moment for a specific purpose. At the time we may not appreciate the reasoning for such a connection, but often later we reflect and understand. Fran Gavey was that person for me, and I will always be grateful for her concern and intervention.

Sometime in the spring of 1999, Fran called me, introducing herself as a member of Dad's congregation at the Cranford United Methodist Church. It seems that Fran's son Brian, Dad's mechanic, had some disturbing news about my father. Apparently Dad had recently walked several miles to Brian's Automotive in Garwood to pick up his car, which he thought he had dropped off for servicing. The car had never been brought in. When I questioned him about this, Dad remarked casually that he had found his car, having *misplaced* it earlier. He seemed surprised that I was worried.

After Fran's warning, I started making more regular visits to Dad, including one overnight per week. Dad and I settled into a routine that spring and summer of 1999, and together we would go grocery shopping, out to lunch, to the Cranford Swim Club and to appointments. I would check to see that his laundry was done and the old dog fed and walked. By this time Randi was blind, deaf, and incontinent, but Dad loved his little buddy and refused to have him put to sleep. I reluctantly respected his wishes. Eventually God took Randi. Nancy Biro, Dad's next-door neighbor, called me when she noticed my father in the backyard with a shovel, trying to dig a grave! Fearing that Dad would forget his beloved dog had died and go off searching for him, I put up signs in his house as a reminder. Eventually he stopped asking about the dog.

During one visit a huge stack of mail was delivered, which Dad tried to hide from me. I discovered that he had been sending checks everywhere in response to pleas for help. I now know that some of these *charities* were fraudulent. When I questioned him, he became quite defensive and said that it was *his* money and that he liked to help people. He showed me a notebook where he carefully recorded each outgoing check. He seemed quite proud and remarked that each contribution was only five or ten dollars. Upon closer inspection, I noticed that he was giving money away to over one hundred causes, often with a check every month to the same organization. Dad was financially assisting such people as Linda Tripp, Paula Jones, and all political parties, as well as numerous religious, police and medical organizations. That money certainly added up, and requests poured in as his name was added to other mailing lists. Dad also entered sweepstakes, tempted by those wonderful prizes to send in even more money. He was delighted by the enticement gifts he received in the mail, including cheap tee shirts, coins, and junky plastic toys. His lack of judgment was a red flag that something was amiss.

One scam involved a chimney-cleaning service. Although Dad's house did not have a fireplace, these people convinced him that he needed to have his chimney cleaned regularly. My husband tracked them down and was able to stop payment on a $1000 check Dad had sent for this unnecessary service. We put signs up in the house that he should not agree to any work done on his house without checking with us first.

One day when I was putting clothes away in his closet, I found grocery bags filled with old mail. Eventually I discovered dozens more bags of mail in other closets and the attic bedroom. It took me many days to sort through this stuff, because important correspondence was interspersed among the junk mail. Over time, this had clearly gotten out of hand, and Dad was quite clever at keeping it hidden from me.

Maybe I should have taken away his checkbook at this point, but he *was* diligent about paying his bills and seemed to enjoy the process of recording his checks and preparing them to be mailed. For decades Mil had been an avid keeper of records. Everyone in the family knew about the stacks of index cards, where he kept lists of everything from the number of times he had mowed the lawn, to the prices of gasoline, to bridge scores over the years. Mom never understood his obsession with those lists, many of which were scribbled in pencil. Knowing how ingrained this recording activity was in Dad, I came up with an idea. I would oversee the writing of his checks, making sure he paid his bills. Then I would offer to mail his letters on my way home. He never knew that I tore up all the mail going to charities and sweepstakes. This worked well for some months, making Mil feel productive and giving me time to process the fact that he was indeed losing not only memory but judgment. Around this time Dr.Toro started Dad on *Aricept*, the best Alzheimer's medication at the time, with a warning that it might not be effective. I was willing to take a chance.

On a hot day in August, 1999, I arrived to find Dad in bed, sweaty and confused. He had forgotten to turn on his central air conditioning. After giving him a drink and helping him into the shower to cool off, he rallied and told me that he had been out looking for his car. I called the Cranford police who informed me that Dad had called them earlier from a store downtown to report that his car was missing. They later found it in a parking space near the train station, where he had apparently left it when going to the dentist earlier in the day. The spaces in front of his dentist's office were all taken, so Dad had parked a couple of blocks away and then forgotten where he left his car. He walked three or four miles home in ninety degree heat! That ended Dad's driving privileges. From then on I enlisted others to take him to church, Old Guard and senior activities. I confiscated three sets of car keys until someone from town informed me that he was seen driving around again. Apparently he had a fourth set, which I took as well.

In October, 1999, Hurricane Floyd dumped two feet of water into Dad's garage and lower level of his split-level house. Nancy waded over to check on Dad until the roads were clear. His old Ford was ruined, which put an end to the driving situation for good. My biggest fear was that Dad would go out walking, looking for his car. I put signs up stating that his car was gone because it no longer worked. From time to time Dad would say he wanted to buy a new car, and I would tell him we would go next month. Eventually he stopped asking.

In retrospect, I wonder if I should have taken away Dad's car keys earlier. Should I have sold his car back in the spring? It would seem so in view of what transpired, but the truth is that I felt in my heart I could not take everything away at once. I know from talking to others with similar situations that you don't react at once to every event that unfolds; rather, it is a process of assimilation. It takes some time to understand that there is a problem with an elderly parent and to plan the next step. I felt pulled into a new role, and I needed to be guided by my heart as well as my head.

My family began to feel more and more uneasy about Dad living alone.

CHAPTER 7

DECISION TIME

Anosmia is the loss of the sense of smell. Dad apparently had this condition for several years. Researchers have found that people with mild cognitive impairment who cannot identify more than two of ten items presented in a sniff test are five times more likely to progress to Alzheimer's disease. I arrived at my father's house one day in 1999 and was greeted by an incredible stench of burnt metal. I found a discarded tea kettle in his kitchen that had been burned right through the bottom. I located Dad napping upstairs, showed him the evidence and asked him what had happened. His reply was, "Oh, I guess I need a new teapot!"

Thoughts of a potential house fire haunted me. After airing out his kitchen, I taped up the stove knobs and left written instructions on how to heat up water in his microwave. I paid a nurse friend to check up on Dad on a regular basis when I couldn't get there. He was looking thinner and maybe even forgetting to eat. He was always sleepy and ready for a nap. A neighbor told me she often saw lights on in his house in the middle of the night.

The signs of dementia, possibly Alzheimer's disease, were slowly adding up: difficulty remembering recent conversations and events; trouble handling tasks that required different steps; decreased ability to reason; and problems finding his way around familiar places. Dad would say, "I'm all mixed up."

Christmas 1999 was a turning point. Lois and Bill drove up from North Carolina to stay with Dad. It was wonderful to see Mil pose happily with some of his grandchildren and great-grandchildren. However, he was thinner than usual and confused at times, so we knew that a decision had to be made quickly for his safety.

Bayada Nurses was able to schedule a certified home health aide, Annette Bennett, to stay with him five days each week starting in January, 2000. This wonderful woman had previously worked on an hourly basis but was willing to try a live-in case. Thankfully, she remained with Dad until the end of his life and provided invaluable care so that he could remain at home. In order to become certified in home care in New Jersey, aides must pass a two-week course. Their skills are checked upon hire at Bayada Nurses and reviewed regularly on supervisory visits in the home.

Since Dad was sleeping so much and losing weight, I contacted his doctor and asked him to make a Hospice referral. Hospice is a concept of palliative rather than curative care for patients who have a limited life expectancy. Many are cancer patients, but anyone is accepted regardless of age or type of illness. The people from Center for Hope Hospice in Linden were wonderfully supportive, but it soon became evident that I was premature in calling them. With Annette's care and cooking, Dad began to gain weight and show some interest in life. Hospice discharged him after ninety days, and they never made me feel that I had contacted them too soon. Three years later Dad and I would re-connect with them at the true end of his life.

Annette, Dad and I settled into a routine. I would pick her up at the Cranford train station early each Monday morning, drive her to Dad's, and then continue on up to my job in Morristown. On Wednesdays, my day off, I would go to Cranford and do his grocery shopping or take him to an appointment. Then on Saturday mornings, I would leave my home in Cedar Knolls, take Annette to the train station and live in with Dad over the weekend. I began to have new respect for live-ins once I became one of them. It is a twenty-four hour a day job, much like being a parent.

Looking back to January – May 2000, I wonder how I was able to work four days a week in my current nursing job, complete my Bachelor of Nursing degree at the College of Saint Elizabeth, care for my father on weekends and maintain my own home. Fortunately, I am blessed with good health and energy. My husband never objected when I told him I wanted to go to Cranford on weekends rather than get a variety of fill-in aides, which usually happens on live-in cases. John played an important role in dealing with financial issues, which were complicated because of Mil's memory problems. For example, we discovered that Dad simply copied the figures from his tax filings from one year to the next. That situation alone took time to unravel. We were able to manage Dad's money so that he could continue to live at home, which was his wish.

Our children, Johnny, a port coordinator for a chemical company, and Kristen, a hospital-employed registered nurse, would take turns driving over to visit their grandfather. Johnny's truck came in handy for cleaning up the yard. Dad somehow always remembered my husband and son by name, referring to them as *his* sons.

Although he knew I was his daughter, he had trouble remembering my name. A possible reason for this is that although my birth name is Claire, I have been known by my nickname Ginger since I was in elementary school. With his memory loss, however, Dad would refer to me by any name that popped into his brain, making me wonder just how many women had been in his life! Kristen's hair color had changed over the years, and when she stopped over, Dad would always ask me, "Who's the little blonde girl?" When I reminded him that she was his youngest grandchild, and *my* baby, he'd say, "How about that!" and then repeat the question. He did love the attention she gave him.

David, a doctor in Seattle, was the first out-of-state grandchild to visit Papa in 2000. He was returning home in March from a trip to Africa, where he had reunited with former Peace Corps friends and helped out in a local hospital. Dad recognized David and was happy to see him. He knew that he had traveled a great distance, but he was unable to process all of his grandson's stories.

Whether you had come from another country or another room did not matter to Dad as his short-term memory loss became more severe. He never remembered who was in the house with him, and he was always surprised when he saw someone there. Mil greeted you as if he hadn't seen you in years, because in his mind, he hadn't!

In the spring and summer of 2000, I took Dad out every weekend. We would go downtown where he could participate in his favorite activity, people-watching. Before his dementia, my father was a courteous gentleman, mannerly and somewhat quiet. Now there was no filter, so his thoughts came right out in words. He made comments about fat people, tall people, women with large breasts, and bearded or bald men. He invariably told men with facial hair "How about a shave?" Once in the pharmacy he walked right up to a well-endowed young woman and told her he liked her breasts! I apologized profusely, but she laughed and said she understood because her grandfather acted the same way. Dad then turned towards a full-figured woman, who was closer to his own age, and complimented her on her lovely blouse. He got approval from me, and the lady seemed charmed by his attention.

Sometimes we would go to the Cranford pool. Once he swam six laps during an adult swim. I was in the water right beside him and finally urged him to stop because he was getting tired. I had quite a time getting him out of the pool, as his legs were getting weak, and I had left his cane by the chair. It was worth it, however, because he was so proud of himself, and I remember that he slept extra well that night. We would sit near the diving boards because they were closer to the bathroom in case Dad had to go there in a hurry. He loved observing each diver, and he was always ready with a comment. He'd call out, "Nice dive, bud!" or "Oh, that was a good trick!" or "Well, I see you didn't lose your suit!" One time he was distracted by the sound of an airplane overhead after a man he was watching dove into the pool. When he looked back at the water, he panicked because he never saw the man re-surface. Dad bolted up from his chair and stepped to the edge of the pool, ready to dive in and save the man! I had all I could do to convince him that the diver had gotten out while he was looking skyward.

I began to wonder just what was happening to Dad's thinking. I came to realize that he was literally trapped in the moment, unable to understand cause and effect. This was the reason for his intense focus on the here and now. The present was what he knew best, and what he saw in front of him became his world. People would come up to him in town and greet him by name. Always polite, Mil would respond in a friendly way, but then turn to me and ask, "Who the hell was that?"

Long-term memory remained intact. He knew his name, that he grew up in Brooklyn, and that he and his wife had moved to New Jersey after their marriage in 1939. He recalled that he went to James Madison High School and that he graduated from Dartmouth College, class of 1931. He remembered the Depression, Pearl Harbor, World War II, and that he was a Republican. When I showed him the memory album presented to him at his retirement, he seemed surprised about his career accomplishments, because all he remembered about his job was that he sat at a desk and looked at some papers.

I found it interesting to learn that in 1910, the year Dad was born, toothpaste cost twenty-five cents, and an average washing machine only $7.15. Thomas Edison demonstrated his latest invention, talking motion pictures, and couples were doing a new dance called *The Tango.* The first airplane flight was made from the deck of a ship in Norfolk, Virginia. President William Howard Taft began the tradition of throwing out the game ball on baseball's opening day. The fact I like most about 1910 is that Father's Day was started in Spokane, Washington. Whenever I mentioned historical facts, Dad would perk up and pay attention. Those he often remembered with incredible clarity.

Although he knew his wife's name was Marion, he would not mention her unless I showed him a picture. Then he would say, "I wonder where she's been lately?" After I'd remind him that she had died, he would be sad for a moment and then shift his attention to something else that he noticed. His mind always returned to the safety and comfort of the present.

On our walks, Dad would occasionally look up at the sky and comment on people he knew who were *up there.* Thinking he wanted to talk about Heaven, I'd ask if he was getting ready to go. Usually he would say in a quite rational tone, "Eventually, but not today." One time, however, he loudly proclaimed, "Who, me? Hell, no!"

As I spent more time with Dad and got to know him in a new way, I realized how much I enjoyed his eccentricity. I began to jot down his amusing remarks and passed these on to family members via weekly e-mails. These reports, which also included caregiving challenges, were called Papa Updates and form the basis for this book. Feedback from these detailed e-mails was mostly encouraging and positive. I know it was therapeutic for me to document my feelings. Reinforcement from my support system gave me the strength to continue on this journey with dementia, even though I did not know where it would lead, or how long it would take. I always had a deep feeling that I was doing the right thing by keeping my father in his own home, and I appreciated those family members who supported me in this endeavor even during the challenging times.

Chapter 8

Activities

Once Dad was safe in his home with live-in care, he began to gain weight and stamina. He still seemed to need a lot of sleep and naps, but when he was awake he was quite alert and interested in his surroundings. From his youth he had a knack with words, and our family enjoyed reading his clever writings and poetry. Since he used to enjoy crossword puzzles, I bought him a book of easy ones and a book of word games. I was thrilled to see him take an interest in these books, hoping their content would activate some brain cells. I soon realized that he was copying the words from the answer sheets at the back of the books. At least this activity kept him busy for awhile. Sadly, as time went on, he was unable to figure out how to cheat, and the puzzles frustrated him.

When the grandchildren were young, they loved playing board games with Papa. I decided to teach him to play *Chutes and Ladders*. He quickly caught on to the strategy, but it soon became evident that he wanted to play it *his* way. He insisted on going *up* the chutes if it advanced his pawn. When I told him he should play by the rules, he pouted like a little kid and said he didn't *like* those rules!

Next we tried playing *Candy Land*. He became upset because he could not differentiate between the orange and pink squares, and between the blue and green. The shades of color in the older version of this game are actually quite similar. It made me wonder whether some children may have had difficulty with this color distinction.

Next I brought out *Scrabble*. While we never actually played the game, I decided to give him letters and see what words he could form. Here is a list of words he made in about ten minutes one day: *work, rice, desert, long, tattoo* (spelled correctly) *dirt, tunnel, jabber* (there's a word you don't hear much today!) *haze, ham, glow, sane, cram*, and *flash*. I was pretty impressed with the variety, and Mil was proud of himself. My excitement was short-lived, however, because as time went on he started spelling other words like *piss* and *shit*. I left him a note by the *Scrabble* box reminding him that these words were not nice, and he responded by forming the following words: *yes, God, wishes, well,* and *hope*. My optimism faded when he returned to naughty words and began to use them over and over. I grew tired of asking him to clean up his act, but occasionally he would surprise me by spelling something nice like *hello, greetings to you!* Clearly he knew the difference!

A wooden puzzle of the United States held his interest for a time. Like a child would do, he always located the bigger states right away. Once I heard him say, "Helloooo, Texas! You are a *big* fella, and I know just where you go!" The square states frustrated him, and he gave up trying to figure out where the small states went. I didn't care if he got it right or not. I was just happy to see him enjoying an activity.

Dad loved watching sports on TV, especially baseball and football. Formerly an avid Brooklyn Dodgers fan, he switched his allegiance to the Mets. Now he rooted for whichever team caught his eye. Although he never seemed to know who was playing, he did remember the rules of the game. He enjoyed shouting to the TV, "Nice catch, Bud!" or "You're *OUT!*" or "Home Run!" He never failed to notice when a pitcher or batter was left-handed. I'd ask which team he was cheering for, and he would reply, "The guys with the blue hats." Football also stirred his memory. I discovered a notebook from the 1930's in which he had made detailed sketches of important plays as he listened to a game on the radio. Now he was amused to watch and yell at the players on TV until he lost interest and took a nap. As he got older, he would fall asleep even during the most exciting game. I would try to arouse him, but he always told me he wasn't sleeping but was just resting his eyes.

For physical stimulation, Annette or I would escort Dad on walks around the neighborhood. Initially he needed a straight cane, which came in handy for batting every little stone or leaf that came his way. He would notice even the tiniest bug that crossed his path and would often bend over to talk to it. He loved imitating animal sounds as we walked along, answering a dog's bark in the same pitch or a bird's chirp on the same note. It was so silly at times that I couldn't stop giggling. I felt as though I was in the company of Mel Blanc, the talented voice of many cartoon characters from years ago.

One cold winter day I remember taking Dad for a walk in a park near my childhood house on Hillcrest Avenue. As we sat together on a bench sharing a bag of jelly beans, I recalled the fun we used to have there picnicking, sledding, or walking our dog Frisky. Dad wasn't interested in my reminiscing. He was intent on watching the squirrels scamper in the snow and run up and down the trees. His focus was always on the present.

Oldest grandson Gary, a biomedical engineer for an international medical device company, visited from California with his wife Marisol in July, 2001. I was happy that my father recognized Gary, who was glad to find him looking so well. Papa flirted with Marisol but was appropriate in his choice of words. The three of them sat on the sofa, and as we talked, Dad amused himself by waving to his reflection in the mirror across the room. Then he would ask Marisol who she was, and she reminded him of his great- grandchildren Anthony, Danielle, and

Brandon. After looking at pictures, he seemed to get the connection, and soon he was back to charming Marisol.

Realizing that I needed an occasional break from my caregiving responsibilities, I presented my sister with a proposition. I would repay all their travel expenses out of Dad's account if she and her husband would take the time to come up from North Carolina for the weekend, preferably once a season. Dad enjoyed their company, as well as visits from some of their New Jersey friends. John and I took advantage of this time to go away on some weekend trips, but I looked forward to returning to my weekends with Dad. One spring Mary Lou and Mike Castoro, John's sister and brother-in-law, came over to stay with my father so that we could attend a wedding. Johnny and Kristen sat with Papa so John and I could go to my company's Christmas parties. Family support is invaluable when caring for loved ones at home, and it is much appreciated.

Eventually, as his legs became weaker, Dad needed a quad cane for balance. He got a kick out of the fact that this cane did not fall over and could stand up by itself. He kept saying, "How about that!" The new cane made it more challenging to swat at objects in his path, but that never stopped him from trying. Fortunately, he did not fall while swinging his cane back and forth, but there were a few close calls.

During the last year of his life he walked with the help of a roller-walker. I got him a bright royal blue one with a basket and small seat. Nothing but the best for the king of Brookdale Road! He was quite happy with the attention he received from people who admired his snazzy new vehicle. If he became tired, I would lock the brakes and let him sit on the seat. Sometimes he would sit too long, cross his long legs, fold his arms and lower his head for a snooze. Then I would have quite a time getting him up again to walk back home. One time he told me to wheel him home, but I did not want to start doing that, because it was not a wheelchair, and the tires were very small. Besides, I knew that exercise was important. If I promised him a beer, he would perk up immediately and was able to walk home pretty fast. When we got home, I would settle him into his easy chair and give him an *O'Doul's* non-alcoholic beer. Soon he'd be loudly singing his favorite German drinking song, *Ein Prosit!* My family clearly remembers the Thanksgiving he burst into this song while I was saying a prayer at the table. With a short attention span, obviously he thought my prayer was too long.

Sometimes we would play catch with a soft, colorful over-sized ball that I ordered from an activities catalog intended for older folks. We'd sit in the living room and toss the ball around, or kick it to each other. After a while, Dad would say, "That's enough of *that!*" and put it behind his head for a pillow. Great granddaughter Casey was a toddler in Christmas 2000, and she and Papa took turns playing with that ball. Once with my daughter Kristen, he noticed that the tag on the ball showed that it had been made in Mexico. He remembered going there, so she asked where else he had traveled. He told her that he had been to Brooklyn, saying, "You should go there. Where do you come from?" When Kristen told him she lived in Kearny, NJ, he immediately recalled that he used to work there, long ago, for Western Electric. We were always fascinated when his mind was able to connect the dots of memory.

An important activity for memory-impaired folks is called *reminiscence therapy.* Nursing homes encourage families to display photos and other memorabilia in rooms as a visible reminder of past events. It became my mission to make Dad's home a *Mil Hallenbeck* living museum. As I cleaned out closets and his attic, I uncovered a treasury of photographs, letters, and yearbooks from his past. His grammar school and high school diplomas were as large and ornate as his degree from Dartmouth, so I had them professionally framed. When I hung them on the wall of his TV room, he would say, "That's *me*? How about that!" Happy memories were rekindled when he looked at his Dartmouth yearbook and college photographs. He was drawn to the beautiful lady in his wedding photo. After reminding him that she was his wife Marion, he'd often remark, "Who is the handsome fella?" He never quite believed that it was him. Other old photographs were framed and set around the house with labels for easier identification.

When he was no longer able to understand complicated sentences or newspaper articles, I had him read children's books. That worked for a while, but eventually even these simple stories held no interest for him. Even comic strips in the Sunday papers no longer made sense to him. Cartoons on TV caught his eye only if they were slow-moving and uncomplicated, like *Winnie the Pooh*. As time went on, his attention span became even shorter, and he would have trouble following any storyline. He frequently commented, "What's this all about?"

I sent away for a big memory board with interchangeable cards for day, date, season, and weather. Dad would look at this while eating at his kitchen table. If we forgot to change the weather card, he would look out the window and let us know if we were wrong. He always expressed amazement at the year. If I asked him what year it was he would invariably say anything from 1940 to 1960.

Granddaughter Bonnie, a former engineer in graduate school for an MBA, traveled to Singapore to see her boyfriend Dan Lawrence and sent postcards for Papa to read. He knew who she was and that Asia was far away. When she returned to Tennessee, she would often send homemade cookies wrapped in colorful boxes. I would describe her grandfather's glee at receiving these gifts. If grandson Steven, an advertising media director in North Carolina phoned, Papa always asked the same question, "Where are you? Do you like it there?" Steve would patiently remind his grandfather about his family and home. He and his wife Debbie kept in touch by sending photos of their children, Casey and Tyler. David sent pictures of his daughter Aurelia and special homemade powder for Papa to use after his shower. Gary, Marisol, Lois and Bill sent goodies and photos. Each week I would repeat the names of Mil's family members and where everyone lived. After reviewing the pictures, his usual comment was that he had a good-looking family. I'd remind him that *he* had started it all!

Music stirred Dad's memory. He would sing along to familiar songs or hymns in a loud, lusty voice. After each selection on the CD he'd yell, "Bravo!" or occasionally in response to an opera singer, "You *stink*, lady!" (Tell us how you really feel, Mil.) *Jesus Loves Me* was a favorite of his, as well as *Row, Row, Row Your Boat*. Sometimes on our walks he would make up little ditties, like "Hi, ho, hi ho, it's on a walk I go," adding: "I use my cane, I do, I do, to help me walk I do!" Once when we were singing *The Farmer in the Dell*, he stopped to ask me, "What's a dell?" There was a time when I was little that I believed my father knew everything. It dawned on me that now he was looking to *me* for answers.

Dad was naturally very sad when I told him about the death of his lady friend Alice in March of 2001. Instead of taking him to the funeral home, I chose to pay our respects at a gathering at her home. Dad did not even recognize her house, although he had been there many times since Mom died. He enjoyed the food and company, and Alice's children and grandchildren were happy to see him. When he was introduced to a woman named Irene, he burst into a rendition of *Good Night, Irene*, which was quite charming. I am sure he forgot why we were even there, because when I mentioned it on the way home, he replied, "Oh, did Alice die?" One of the blessings of memory loss is that you cannot recall sad events for long.

In addition to a wonderful singing voice, Dad had great rhythm. He loved to clap his hands, slap his thighs, and tap his feet to any tune, real or imagined. He would keep the beat while watching TV shows with musical numbers. He could vocally imitate the sound of just about any instrument he heard with incredible accuracy. He loved parades! All those wonderful musical sounds in a parade on TV kept him quite busy.

I loved to hear my father play the accordion when I was a little girl. I retrieved the instrument from the closet one day and helped him into the straps. The poor guy nearly fell over when he stood up and tried to coordinate the keyboard and the bellows! We tried it again while sitting down, but his knees kept getting caught as he attempted to play. He was more successful with his harmonica. He played the same songs over and over, always ending with *Shave and A Haircut: Two Bits!* His repertoire consisted of *Swanee River, Polly Wolly Doodle*, and *I've Been Workin' on the Railroad.* I figured this activity was good for breath control as well as mental stimulation. Once in the middle of the night I was awakened by one of his renditions, followed by Mil enthusiastically clapping for himself. How wonderful to be able to keep yourself so entertained!

I am by nature very energetic and react quickly in most situations. During his last years my father did everything very slowly, so it took time for me to adjust to his lack of speed. It reminded me of the children's story comparing a tortoise and hare. As the weeks and months passed, I began to relax and enjoy the peace and quiet of my weekends with Mil. The phone rarely rang, he napped a lot, and often I would find myself dozing on his sofa with a book propped open on my stomach. These rest periods helped fortify me for his nighttime awakenings. I experienced a heightened awareness of the present and began noticing things with Dad, like the sunlight streaming in and reflecting objects. He reacted with childlike wonder at a rainbow dancing on the ceiling as the sun passed over my mother's etched glass box on the coffee table. I was learning to slow down and appreciate being in the here and now. It was a welcome change from my normally hectic pace of life, and I felt at peace.

CHAPTER 9

BIRTHDAYS

I have heard it said that the prospect of death grows friendlier as we grow older, but with Mil's dementia, he seemed to be optimistic about life. His ninetieth birthday party in September, 2000, was quite an event. Both daughters and sons-in-law, and two of his six grandchildren were able to attend, as well as neighbors and friends, including Dr. Barrie Smith, his minister. Bonnie and Johnny gave Papa special attention and helped him blow out all ninety candles. With childlike joy he smiled at the balloons and decorations, which I kept up for days afterward. Dad told me after the party that life was good! Like a little kid, he tried to sneak too many candies and cookies, so Annette and I had to keep the leftovers hidden.

Some days when asked about his age, Dad would say he was "around a hundred and fifty" which probably revealed how he felt at the moment. Another time he would express amazement when told his age. His boyhood friend Claude Grady called from Florida to say that after ninety, it was all downhill. Mil quickly rejected that idea.

His ninety-first birthday party was smaller, and he was showing signs of slowing down. At one point during the gathering, I whispered to him if he knew why all those people were here, and he answered, "I have no idea." Still, his good manners prevailed, and he charmed everyone and seemed to enjoy the attention of his special day. Later, after his nap, all memory of this event was erased. The balloons and signs were again kept up as a visual reminder.

God is merciful! I am grateful I didn't know in late September, 2002, that we would be celebrating Dad's last earthly birthday. His party consisted of a few neighbors, John and me. People began arriving while I was upstairs fussing to make Dad presentable. As I escorted him down the hall to the short flight of stairs, he peered ahead and commented, "What the hell is going on?" Soon he was all smiles when he realized that the gathering was for him. I even encouraged everyone to become involved in a game of catch with his giant soft ball. Shouldn't every birthday boy have a party game?

The following day was his actual birthday, Sunday, September 22. We slowly walked into church with a helium balloon tied to his roller-walker. I wanted to make sure my father was noticed, and soon he was receiving lots of good wishes. Jim Silkensen, one of Dad's neighbors, was lay minister that day. He led the congregation in singing *Happy Birthday* to Dad. While everyone sang *Amazing Grace*, he turned to me and sang his own version, "Amazing *me!* I'm ninety-two!" The Baldwins visited later that day after Dad's nap. Dick, a Dartmouth alumnus, had just been to a reunion at the college and showed us some recent photos. I brought out old college snapshots to add to the memory-sharing. Dad was alert and interested.

Birthdays are special events for everyone, regardless of age. I treasure the memory of my father's joy celebrating this last birthday.

CHAPTER 10

EXCURSIONS

Rides in the car became important events for Dad. We usually didn't go far, just downtown to appointments, or to have his hair cut. He struggled to fit those long legs into my car, but once inside he would become excited. As we traveled along Riverside Drive, he always made a comment about the winding river we passed. For many months it was the same remark, even in summer, "No ice on the river!" Then one day he switched to, "Stop here! I want to take a swim!" Every time we passed the river, he'd make that same statement, over and over, looking to me for a reaction. When we passed a jogger or someone taking a walk, he would tap on his window and say, "Hello!" Invariably, these people were too absorbed in their thoughts to notice an old man waving. Sometimes Dad would mutter, "Unfriendly bastard!" He could never understand why the world wasn't friendly. Once while we were stopped at a red light, Dad put his window down and shouted to the woman driver next to him, "I like your lipstick, lady!" She looked surprised but at least gave him a smile, which made his day. He liked pushing the window button up and down, like a little kid. When we had things to mail at the post office, I'd drive up to the outside mailbox and give him the task of putting letters into the slot. After thanking him, I'd always get the same reply, "I try to be helpful!"

He enjoyed making phrases out of the letters he noticed on license plates. *JCH* became *Jesus, come here!* and *KCN* stood for *Kiss...come near!* Car games provide amusement for children of all ages, even in their nineties. He got a kick out of rain on the windshield or window washing fluid squirting on the glass. Simple things that were in his direct line of vision caught his attention.

McDonald's and *Burger King* were favorite places to take my father, because he could watch the children play while we ate. He especially loved it when kids jumped into the pool of colorful balls. I'll bet he wished he could join them. Whenever employees swept the floor near our table or set out condiments, he would comment on what a good job they were doing. I am sure that most people never compliment these workers. Dad always made them smile, and that made him happy.

Getting Dad out to see doctors became more challenging as time went on and his legs became less stable. I can clearly recall when Annette and I were trying to get him ready for an appointment at the eye doctor's. He protested, saying that he did not need to have his *body* washed if only his *eyes* were being examined. In the waiting room, he sat next to a beautiful young woman wearing a tube top. He began complimenting her on her toenail polish. As his eyes began to wander upward over her body, I whispered to him to please be a gentleman. He then told her, "My daughter is always giving me helpful hints!" The eye exam was a little tricky, because he could not remember the instructions. His ophthalmologist had no explanation for Dad's ability to read fine print with his *distance* glasses! This is an example of how little we know about the perception of a brain afflicted with dementia.

Dad's podiatrist, Dr. Sabeh, had to endure armpit tickles from his patient's feet as he tried to cut his toenails. Mrs. Sabeh was his office assistant, and she was always pleasant towards my father. I had to signal her to hide the candy dish when we arrived, or Dad would grab a handful of treats and later have a stomach ache. I appreciated the kindness and understanding shown by this couple.

Dr. Toro, Dad's primary care physician, treated him with great respect. Dad was fascinated with the doctor's neckties and repeatedly complimented him on his selection. When having his heart examined, he would inquire, "Am I alive?" While waiting for his examination, he would tap his foot on the metal table or read the doctor's certificates on the wall and ask me, "What's this all about?" When a nurse entered the room, he would struggle to sit up so that he could begin flirting. Mil's *EKG's* and vital signs were always within normal parameters. Severe scoliosis shortened his once tall frame, but thankfully the pain and stiffness from spinal osteoarthritis were forgotten once he developed dementia. In 1984 Dad had been diagnosed with atrial flutter, but that condition was no longer evident now, and his only heart medication was a low dose of *Lanoxin*. I always consulted with my nephew David as a second opinion for medical matters. His advice and support were invaluable to me during this journey. I am also grateful to him for providing a chapter at the end of this book which offers information for families dealing with Alzheimer's disease.

Dr. Rodman, Dad's dentist, was very kind and patient. Dad suffered from *vasomotor rhinitis,* resulting in chronic post-nasal drip, which was especially challenging in the dental chair. After a few minutes on his back, he would yell, "I'm *choking!*" The dentist would raise his head, reassure him that he was okay, and then quickly resume the cleaning and check-up. All his good care paid off, because at the age of ninety-two, Dad was missing only one tooth.

I have many great memories of our trips to the barbershop. There were four Italian barbers in Cranford who made a great fuss whenever Dad entered the shop. He never minded waiting his turn as long as he could watch people. He would turn to me, grin, and inform me that he wasn't getting a haircut, he was getting *all his hairs cut!* Silly Mil. Often, the barbers would have Italian music playing loudly over the speakers. Once Dad burst into song to match the notes phonetically, and a barber asked me, "Is your papa Italian?" One time a customer came into the barbershop wearing a Dartmouth sweatshirt. My father got up quickly, went up to the man and shouted the Dartmouth College Indian war cry: *WAHOOWAH!*

While sitting in the barber chair, Dad would amuse himself by sticking out his tongue and making faces in the mirror. Once he frowned and told me he did not like that old man. Sometimes his reflection would scare him or make him sad. I wonder if he realized that it was his image. Maybe in his childlike state he was looking for a child's face to be in that mirror.

I took Dad downtown to see Santa one Christmas when his legs were still strong. Santa good-naturedly spent time with him, asking if he had been a good boy all year.

Assuring him that he had, Dad then struck up a conversation with one of the reindeer and let me take a photo of them all. Back home in his attic, I found a picture taken in 1913 of my father on a pony next to Saint Nick. Uncle Sherrill Newton, my mother's brother, told me that every Christmas when they were little, a photographer went door-to-door in Brooklyn, soliciting parents to pay for these photos. A winter backdrop was included to add authenticity. This gave me an idea for his Christmas card that year. I made copies of the childhood photo and wrote *I still believe in Santa ~ Merry Christmas!* next to Mil's signature. He enjoyed looking at the picture, but he was not convinced that the cute baby was really him.

With Saint Nick in 1913

Still enjoying Santa at age 90

**Mil singing bass in the
Cranford United Methodist Church Choir
Cranford, NJ**

**Young Millard in the
Ocean Ave. Congregational Church Choir
Brooklyn, NY**

Marion and Mil in 1938

Dad and his Bathing Beauties Circa 1950

Dad (far right)
Negotiating military contracts
for Bell Laboratories, 1974

Papa and Great-Granddaughter, Casey, sharing a toy

The birthday boy at 90 with daughters Lois (left) and Ginger

A major trip for Dad was the half-hour ride to our home in Cedar Knolls for the Thanksgiving and Christmas holidays. He never stopped looking out the car windows at the passing scenery and chatting about everything he saw. It was tricky getting him up my long sidewalk, but we were able to manage this with John's help. Sadly, Dad had no recollection of ever having been in my home. I set up a bed in the living room and a baby gate at the bottom of the stairs leading to the second floor. It was good to have him with us, but in this different environment, he was more confused than usual. One night after supper, he pushed his chair away from the table, thanked us for our hospitality, and went to the front door. He said his mother was worried about him, and he needed to go home. It was a cold night, so he quickly came back inside when I told him I had dessert.

Another time we caught him trying to unhook the baby gate. Johnny asked his grandfather where he was going, and Papa replied that he was going upstairs to get his cigarettes. When I reminded him that he didn't smoke anymore, he replied, "That's what *you* think!" The good thing about Dad's dementia was that he could be distracted from an unsafe situation by the offer of food or a beer. He could easily have fallen that night on my steep stairs looking for a smoke.

Since there was no shower on the first floor in my home, I had to give him a sponge bath when he stayed with us. Once Kristen and I decided to give him a thorough soaping up in the laundry room, while he stood holding on to the washtub. We nurses worked as quickly and efficiently as possible in spite of his protests. He would yell, "What the hell is going on down there?" By the time we had him all cleaned, lotioned, powdered and into fresh pajamas, we assumed he felt refreshed. Kristen asked him if he felt better, but he replied loudly, "NO!" Still, he gave her a big hug.

As time went on, excursions outside his home became fewer and fewer. The world my father once knew became smaller and smaller. He could not remember traveling to different countries with my mother after his retirement, even when I showed him the detailed notes he had taken of these trips. Fortunately, journals of these vacations have been handed down to family members, so that we are able to re-live the joy Mil once felt when his world was vast and his memory intact.

CHAPTER 11

CHURCH

Church attendance was always important to my father. He joined the Cranford United Methodist Church on his thirty-sixth birthday, September 22, 1946, and he was a faithful member until the end of his life. I made every effort to take him each Sunday morning in his final years. I had been baptized, confirmed and married there, and it felt good to return to that welcoming place. As time went on it became more difficult to get him up and dressed, but I knew it was worth the effort. People were always happy to see him, and he really enjoyed the worship experience and socialization.

Getting him out of bed was quite a challenge! On most other days he was allowed to stay in bed all morning. On Sundays I would get myself ready first before trying to awaken his lordship. Whenever I asked Dad if he wanted to go to church, his answer was a resounding "Yes!" but then he would invariably turn over in bed and close his eyes. Next I would give him a glass of orange juice, and soon after drinking that, he would get up to use the bathroom. Then I would spring into action, quickly making his bed and laying out his clothes on top. When he returned from the bathroom, he'd see the clothes and remark, "I must be going somewhere!" As he became older and weaker, he would need more assistance getting dressed. I had him tie his necktie as long as he was able, and when he could no longer manage this, I did it for him. Helping him into his socks was tricky, because like little children often do, Mil would curl his toes. If I got frustrated, he would pat me on the head and tell me that he knew I was trying. After struggling to get his feet into his dress shoes, I'd often remark that I was glad he only had two feet. Once he said, "I'm glad I'm not a *quadruped!*" Those Dartmouth professors would have been proud of his vocabulary. His flair for words made me smile.

By the time breakfast was finished and we were getting into the car, Dad forgot where we were going. However, as soon as we passed under the railroad bridge in the center of town and drove on to Walnut Avenue, he began to show excitement, remarking, "My church is around here!" Then he would ask over and over if I had his offering envelope.

I loved walking into church with my father. He was one of the few men who wore a suit and tie, even in summer. I made sure that his outfits were color-coordinated and that he was neatly dressed. When he sang in the choir, I would help him into his robe. Another chorister would always help him with his music. I sat in the back of the church right in his line of vision, and often he would wave to me. Dad's spot in the choir was back row, middle, just underneath a big cross set on red cloth. It was an impressive framing for such a special man, and he looked quite holy.

Unfortunately, Dad's behavior was not always angelic. He thought it was funny to put coins down the backs of the women sitting in front of him, so I had to empty his pockets before church. Then he started tugging on the ladies' dangling earrings or blowing on their necks! Eventually I pulled him out of the choir because he was no longer able to pay attention. The rest of the choir would be standing up to sing, and Mil would be seated, watching the ceiling fan or blowing his nose.

I was also concerned that he might trip on his robe while climbing the stairs to the choir loft. Soon he forgot all about singing in the choir, unless someone reminded him. I loved having him sit next to me in church, especially when we sang hymns. He would embellish the ends of phrases in a loud voice that often made me giggle. One time Dad began to pull the hymnal we both shared away from me, offering it to an attractive young lady on his other side. She did not seem to notice me at all but was clearly charmed by my father. Once when he was about to sign the attendance pad, he looked at me and said, "Marion?" I told him that I was Ginger, and he wrote *Mil and Ginger Hallenbeck.* I guess by then he thought of us as a couple.

He responded with great enthusiasm whenever there were congregational readings, particularly with the words *Lord, Christ, or Jesus.* During sermons, Mil would occasionally shout *Hallelujah!* or *Amen!* Dr. Barrie Smith never seemed to mind, and sometimes he would respond with, "That's right, Mil!" When announcing Dad's death to the congregation, Barrie said that he had lost his *Hallelujah Man.* After any musical performance, my father would shout *Bravo!* I never felt that this disturbed anyone. I was very grateful that his church respected him in his present state of mind and did not find his behavior embarrassing.

Even with his wobbly legs, Dad managed to kneel at the communion rail and get back up without falling. I am certain God gave him a little extra strength when needed. He seemed to remember this sacrament and behaved in an appropriate manner. Sadly, he often forgot that we had taken communion and would ask me when it would be our turn.

Like a mother watching her child, I had to keep an eye on Dad when he became bored in church. He would start kicking the pew with his wing-tip shoes, softly at first, but soon building up to a loud *tap, tap, TAP!* I would put my hand on his knee and whisper for him to stop. If we sat behind a bald man, Dad would tap on his head and comment on the money he must save at the barber's. Of course, I always got nervous if my father was near an ample-breasted woman. I would tilt his chin up and remind him to be a gentleman. Then he would compliment her on her pretty eyes, much to my relief. Once during coffee hour, he told someone he had known for years that she had a nice behind! When I apologized to her, she told me not to worry, as it was just Dad's *id* coming out! (Check Freud for an explanation.)

There were times when I felt an overwhelming heaviness in my heart as I witnessed my father's mental and physical decline. Seeing him so happy in his wonderful church and hearing him sing familiar hymns with such gusto restored the joy in my heart and gave me strength. During requests for prayers he once shouted, "Thank you, God for *everything!*" I was proud of my father for reminding all of us to be so grateful. His mind and body may have been weak, but his spirit was remarkably vital.

CHAPTER 12

9/11

None of us will ever forget the horror of September 11, 2001. The suicide plane attacks on the World Trade Center particularly affected areas close to New York City. Two families on my father's street in Cranford, New Jersey, lost loved ones in this tragedy. Whenever Dad saw the images of that fateful day on TV, he reacted as though it had just happened, because in his mind he was seeing it for the first time. We tried to protect him from this as much as possible.

I asked him if he remembered the attack on Pearl Harbor in 1941, which of course he did, since much of his long-term memory was intact. I then explained this new attack on our country and asked him to consider which was worse. Without hesitation, he replied, "This is worse because it happened right here." Even with his dementia, he could figure that out.

The Sunday after 9/11, a member of Dad's church, Michael Hingson, spoke to a hushed congregation about his experience climbing down seventy-eight stories in the first tower after it had been hit. What made the story even more exceptional was that Michael is blind, and he descended the smoke-filled stairs with his seeing-eye dog, Roselle. I am not sure that Dad could fully comprehend this businessman's account of that hellish day, but he was thrilled to see a dog in church and enjoyed petting her after the service.

Flags were displayed everywhere in Cranford. Dad asked me repeatedly if a parade was coming or if it was the fourth of July. Rather than upset him all over again with the truth, I told him that his town was very patriotic. He seemed to accept this explanation and saluted each flag we passed.

At the conclusion of a Christmas concert later that year, a policeman marched down the aisle carrying a flag to honor the six men from Cranford who were killed on 9/11. Dad was one of the first to stand up and salute. Patriotism is something Mil never forgot, and I was proud of him.

CHAPTER 13

WATCHING THE WORKERS

Dad's house was a four-bedroom split level, built in 1956. He was the original owner. Over the years it had begun to look somewhat shabby, so I started hiring people to make improvements. A landscaper planted shrubs, maintained the lawn, cleared the leaves, and plowed the driveway when it snowed. Mil loved to watch these men work. He would tap on the window and wave to them, shouting "Good Job!" I had to remind them to look up at the house for my father, who could not understand when they didn't wave back. When it snowed or the leaves piled up, we had all we could do to prevent him from going outside. He had shoveled snow and raked leaves well into his eighties, and he thought he needed to continue doing these jobs now.

When the gutter man worked, Dad was in his glory, walking from window to window, following the man's ladder and enjoying the shower of colorful leaves. Power- washing and staining his deck provided hours' worth of entertainment, as did tree- trimming. Dad helpfully warned "Watch out, Bud!" as branches fell to the ground.

One morning a tile man was replacing a cracked marble door saddle in the master bathroom. As usual, Dad was still in bed. Soon he was tapping out a rhythm with his hand on the nightstand that exactly matched the workman's hammering. The tile guy got a kick out of that and began to tell us about his own father who lived until he was ninety-four. It seems that everyone has a story to tell, if only we will take the time to listen.

Other stimulating days for Mil included the installation of a new garage door, furnace and central air conditioner. These were noisy jobs, prompting him to mutter, "What the hell is going on in my house?" As soon as he saw the activity, he became friendly and greeted the workmen. He could not remember what caused the big dent in his old garage door, but I suspect he rammed into it with his car before he stopped driving.

There were several plumbing problems in the house. Not wanting to spend Dad's money remodeling bathrooms, I had the toilet insides replaced as well as many pipes and faucets. That way at least everything flushed and flowed. One time the pipe out to his street backed up, providing some fresh excitement. Since my father's financial point of reference was somewhere around Depression era prices, I told him each job cost around $20. That seemed reasonable to Mil. If he only knew!

The biggest upheaval occurred when I had all the rooms in his house painted off-white. The task was enormous, requiring taking down curtains, dozens of pictures from the walls, and moving furniture. Each day for a week a group of painters arrived, and Dad was very excited with all this activity. He amused himself by reading aloud the words on their tee shirts and telling them that they were doing a good job. Annette had to keep moving him to different rooms so he wouldn't get in their way or fall.

When it came time to have the outside of the house painted, I knew I could not change the color. Dad always knew he lived in a red house, even with his dementia. As time went on, when we sat on his deck out back, he would not recognize his own house. He would say to me, "This is a nice house you have here!" This bothered me until I remembered that it was Mom who wanted the deck built. After she died in 1990, Dad never used it until I moved in on weekends. Right until the end of his life he was able to identify the front of his house, probably because he saw it more often than the back. He also recognized the street on which he lived.

Before the house was painted, it needed to be power-washed. Talk about noise! It sounded as though the world was coming to an end. Mil really got his exercise that time, as he walked around the house trying to follow the commotion.

Ruth was Dad's faithful cleaning lady. She knew him before his confusion set in, and he loved to watch her work. Of course, Annette and I had to keep moving him from room to room so that she could do her job. Each time she came in sight, he greeted her with a big smile and complimented her on her work. When she was finished, I would take her back to the train station, and she would tell me how well Dad looked and remind me that I should be grateful I still had him around.

Annette knew she could always count on Dad's next-door neighbors, Nancy and Joe, during the time when I wasn't there. On more than one occasion Nancy ran over in the night because Annette needed her for a household emergency. You just never know with an older house when something will break down. Maintenance of a house is something that must be considered when you decide to care for someone at home. Dad was very fortunate to have such great neighbors, and I appreciated their willingness to help. Dad, thankfully, slept through these incidents at night. During the day, he enjoyed watching Joe work in his yard. Instead of resting, he would often kneel on his bed and tap on the window to get Joe's attention. Sometimes it's even hard for a big kid to settle down and take his nap!

CHAPTER 14

HALLELUJAH, I'M A BUM!

One of the challenges of caring for a person with dementia is dealing with a condition called *sundowning*. This refers to increased confusion and restlessness at the end of the day and into the night. Much has been written about this phenomenon, but we are still unsure why it occurs. Some patients become so agitated at night that they wander around, searching for something that they are unable to identify. Once Annette found my father anxiously going through his bureau drawers in the middle of the night. She asked what he was doing, and he replied that he wanted to go home, where he was needed. Another time he went to the front door in the middle of the night and opened it, but he told himself out loud that it was cold and dark and came back inside. Confused patients have been known to walk outside and get lost, but fortunately Dad lacked the stamina to do this.

There were nights when he was quite awake, walking to the kitchen and calling out, "Food...I want FOOD!" Usually he would take the snack we left for him and eventually return to bed. Sometimes, however, he would tap his cane loudly on the kitchen floor, clap his hands or yell, "Ho ho ho!" in a loud voice. On weekends I would listen to him for a while and then go downstairs to remind him to go back to bed. Of course, he was always surprised to see me there, because he had forgotten he was not alone. Invariably he would remark, "Oh, did I disturb you?" He looked so innocent at times.

Dad's sneezes were always lusty. I think they even frightened him. He would talk to himself after a loud sneeze, saying, "Shut up, noisy Mil!" Sometimes as he lay in bed he would call out, "Goodnight, my dear!" or "Goodnight, sweetheart!" I thought maybe he was talking to Marion in Heaven, but he told me he was speaking to "anyone who will listen." Sorry, Mom! Other favorite nighttime soliloquies included "Don't let the bedbugs bite...or I'll bite 'em back," and "I am a *liar* in my bed...and that's the *truth!*" He did seem to enjoy talking to himself.

Of all the things Dad shouted, the one we will remember most is "Hallelujah, I'm a bum!" Sometimes he would add, "bum again." He said this repeatedly, almost until the very end of his life. Often he would tell us that *he* was nothing but a "lazy bum." We speculated on the origin of his favorite phrase. Kristen thought it may have come from a book Papa had about his favorite baseball team, the Brooklyn Dodgers, who apparently were also known as *dem bums*. However, it was Bonnie who came up with the answer. Apparently, *Hallelujah, I'm a Bum!* was a union song from the 1890's and later, during the Great Depression, it became a musical starring Al Jolson. This made sense. Dad often referred to himself as a lazy bum because he loved his bed so much, and the Depression years were still very much a part of his personal history. I only wish I had been able to show him the DVD of the musical before he died. How he would have enjoyed that!

CHAPTER 15

BEDBOUND

Time slowly marched on. Dad's walks in the neighborhood became shorter and slower. Everything he did seemed to take more effort, and he slept more and more. His voice remained strong, and he always spoke quite clearly on the phone, belying his physical frailty. Joan Grady called to tell us that her father Claude had died in late August, 2002. Dad was saddened by this news, saying, "Oh, no, I've lost my childhood buddy." They had enjoyed their monthly phone conversations, and I was grateful that Claude remained patient when Mil asked the same questions over and over.

Dad seemed quite comfortable and only rarely complained of hip pain, which was self-limiting. Annette and I managed his bowel urgency with adult pull-up pants, and despite loud protests from Mil, we kept his skin conditioned with lotion. He hated to take a shower, and we decided that two a week were sufficient. A grab bar, shower chair, and hand-held shower head made this process a little easier. His appetite and fluid intake remained good, although each meal took at least an hour for him to consume.

With aging comes an increased risk for falls, which can result in fractures. Sometimes people fall as a result of brittle bones, which my father did not have. Dad was extremely cautious when he walked. He would hold onto the hallway and stairway railings, telling himself, "Don't fall, Mil...one step at a time." He had always been a good walker, which probably added to his longevity. Still, he did fall, and after that everything changed.

Annette rarely needed to call me during the week, because I trusted her to manage Dad's routine. When she phoned me one suppertime late in October 2002, I knew something was wrong. She reported that his hands were quite shaky as he ate, and he seemed even more tired than usual. I instructed her to put him to bed early and call if anything changed. In the middle of the night, she phoned to say that he was on the floor next to his bed, conversing and not in any noticeable discomfort. John and I rushed over to Cranford.

When we arrived, Dad lifted his head up from the pillow Annette had given him, waved, and said, "Hello, John!" I assessed him for injuries and took his vital signs.

Although he appeared to be unhurt, he was unable to stand. We assisted him first to a footstool and then into bed, with John doing most of the lifting. As we turned to leave, we heard Dad shout, "Hallelujah, I'm a bum!"

From this point on, Dad lost all interest in walking. He loved being in bed and having meals brought to him. Then he would nap until we disturbed him in order to provide care. I called Dr. Toro who once again made the recommendation for Hospice. Since Mil's information was already in their system from January 2000, the process was expedited. A social worker, nurse, and physician came out the next day from Center for Hope Hospice in Linden, and Dad was happy with their attention. That evening his hospital bed arrived, which Annette and I set up in the living room next to the big picture window. We re-arranged furniture and wheeled the bed into a position that would allow Dad to have the best view of the neighborhood. The next challenge was how to get him moved downstairs. I called the Cranford First Aid Squad, but their ambulances were out on call. They sent firemen instead, complete with a fire truck which alarmed the neighbors. Poor Dad was scared when the men strapped him into a gurney. I asked them to free his arms so that he could hold onto both hand rails as they carried him down the stairs. This gave him a sense of control. I was grateful that the firemen were gentle with their precious cargo. As Annette and I got our patient settled into his new bed, the men left. I opened the drapes and had Dad wave to them as they drove away. Like a little kid, he seemed excited to watch the big red fire truck.

Annette and I were as nervous as new mothers that night, and we were unable to sleep. We were afraid that he might get confused and try to get out of bed, but Dad did just fine in his new environment. He tried to get up one day when the doorbell rang, so John disconnected it. Mil accepted his bedbound status and seemed grateful for the extra rest. He could turn himself and bend his knees, but he chose not to use his legs for standing and walking.

Now we were in a challenging new phase of Dad's home care. I knew as a nurse that staying in bed could lead to pressure ulcers, commonly known as bedsores. I also knew that Dad would be frightened if placed in a mechanical lift. He even became fearful when we tried to dangle his legs over the side of the bed. Fortunately, Hospice sent a wonderful male aide, Joe, who was able at first to get him out of bed and *dance* him over to an easy chair. On Thanksgiving John and Johnny assisted him to the chair, but Dad soon pleaded with them to put him back to bed.

Hattie, another experienced home health aide from Bayada Nurses, continued to give Dad good bedside care when Annette took time off to be with her family. She handled his inappropriate comments about her body by reminding him that his wife was looking down from Heaven. Mil would look upward and say, "I'm sorry, hon!" but then he would start all over again with his observations. At least the Hospice nun was spared his comments because she was small-figured, although he kept asking her if she had any children.

At one point Dad had not voided in twenty-four hours, so a Hospice nurse inserted a urinary catheter. At first he did not realize it was there. Eventually, though, Dad pulled this out, and I requested that it not be re-inserted. Occasionally, Dad would get agitated and need *Ativan* to calm down. He especially hated being pulled up in bed, hollering, "That's enough of *that*!" loud enough for the entire neighborhood to hear.

During the day, we would leave the drapes open so that he could observe the activities outside. If his neighbors saw him sitting up in his bed they would wave. Mil enjoyed this act of friendliness and especially loved it when someone walked by with a dog. He was happy to watch squirrels run up and down the trees and scamper through the leaves. Sometimes he would look in the other direction across the room to the dining room window. He noticed the big thermometer outside and would ask how cold it was. I propped his big memory board onto a chair so that he could refer to it for information.

Between Dad's bed and the window was a narrow stereo cabinet on which I placed his wedding picture, a small TV, and a note reminding him that he was in his living room. As time went on, he lost interest in television, so we turned on the radio or played CD's. At bedtime I left the radio on to a Christian station which softly played hymns and gave Bible readings. I could hear him in the night saying, "Amen!" and "Yes, Lord!" Maybe he thought God was speaking directly to him. Perhaps He was.

Barrie Smith made wonderful pastoral visits and arranged for ladies in the church to take turns sitting with Dad so that I could do the grocery shopping on Sunday afternoons. Mil shamelessly flirted with these understanding women including Judy, Barrie's wife. Since the fall, many people sent get well cards, and he enjoyed looking at these again and again. I missed taking him to church but am so grateful that the church came to him.

I noticed that after his fall Dad was using his left hand more than his dominant right, and that he had trouble at first playing his harmonica. He also had some difficulty swallowing at times. He probably had a small stroke. Thankfully I did not send him to the hospital after the incident, knowing that this would only add to his confusion. Here at home he was safe and stable, instead of being stuck with IV's and subjected to tests.

I recall learning somewhere that we are all born with only two fears – that of loud noise and that of falling. All other fears are learned as we go through our growth and development. Interestingly, I observed that my father experienced these two fears as he approached the end of his life. Loud noises would startle him in a profound way, and he was extremely afraid of falling when we tried to dangle his legs or have him stand. It somehow seemed appropriate that he revert back to these primal fears in order to complete the circle of life.

Steve came up from North Carolina on a business trip that December and was able to spend time with his grandfather. He enjoyed his visit and noticed Papa's childlike wonder at watching an early snowfall. Seeing this reaction reminded me that we all should take the time to slow down and really focus on the beauty of nature.

Eventually Dad became too weak to feed himself. I asked him then if he wanted to eat and he would say, "Sure! I'm hungry." I told him that as long as his mouth worked, we would feed him. He thought that was a good idea. Sometimes I would get him to open his mouth by saying "Ahhhh." Then he would look at me, smile and say,   "MEN!" Brushing teeth even became too much for him. I started using those tiny breath freshener strips, which he allowed me to place on his tongue. After I'd attend to his personal needs, he'd say, "Let me go to bed!" After being reminded that he *was* in bed, he'd fold his arms and remark, "Good. Now *get lost!*" Relishing in his sleep and naps, he became the most contented bedbound patient I had ever met.

Family members continued to call him, but he had trouble holding the phone or staying awake for a conversation. I thought again about how Mil's world had been shrinking over the years, from traveling all over to being confined to bed. I also noticed that the outside world held less interest for him as he began his final journey.

Although I became apprehensive about what would happen next, he sure looked as though he hadn't a care in the world.

CHAPTER 16

"I'm Going To Die Soon."

In my December 23, 2002, Papa Update I reported to my family that Mil announced that his end was near. I have talked to Hospice nurses who say that terminally ill patients often know when they are going to die. I wondered if this held true for people with dementia. Thinking that my father was just making a silly remark, I replied, "Not at Christmas, I hope!" Dad folded his arms, closed his eyes and said calmly, "No, I'll wait 'til New Year's."

At the time I did not take his premonition seriously because he still ate fairly well, was easily aroused from sleep, and his vital signs were good. I was pleasantly surprised that he remembered that New Year's came after Christmas. He seemed to enjoy looking at the little Christmas tree and other decorations I set up in his new living space. I placed a solar-powered crystal in his window that would rotate in sunlight and make rainbows on the ceiling. He watched this and seemed amused. TV held little interest for him. He slept more and more.

He suffered skin breakdown from an incompetent fill-in aide who worked over Christmas. I agonized over this betrayal. Fortunately, with quick intervention from the Hospice nurses and conscientious care from Annette, his skin healed.

New Year's came and went, and I forgot about Dad's prediction. However, with each passing day, he became weaker and weaker. Everything was an effort for him, and his eyes looked tired. He would stare up at the ceiling for long periods of time. He barely ate, and his perpetually drippy nose dried up. He lacked the energy to suck on a straw, so we fed him liquids with a small spoon. He had to be coached to swallow. One part of me wanted his suffering to be over, yet for selfish reasons I wished that he would never leave me.

The night of January 4, 2003, he yelled out at the top of his lungs two or three times each hour. It was a gut-wrenching howl. I gave him *Ativan*, and he settled down for a while. The next night it happened again, but with less frequency. I would rush to his bed to find him snoring and peaceful. I have no idea what this meant, unless someone was calling him from the other side and he was protesting. I would talk to him and assure him that we loved him, and he would give me the sweetest smile. Annette told me at his memorial service that she often slept on his living room sofa in his final days, just in case he needed her. I will always be grateful for her help and vigilance.

Nothing can prepare you for the death of a loved one. No matter how old you are when you lose your parents, the finality of it hurts in a profound way. My mother's death was sudden and unexpected, but my father's demise was gradual, giving me a lot of time to get to know him better. I lost Dad a bit at a time, which hurt my heart in spurts of sadness. I am not sure which type of grief is worse; I only know that they are just different. When Mom died, we never had time to say *goodbye*. With Dad, it seemed that the *goodbye* part would never end, because we lost him a little piece at a time.

I never dreamed when I was a little girl that I would wind up parenting my father at the end of his life. I always believed that he would protect me forever. How ironic life can be! I also know that he never planned on behaving like a child, sometimes acting silly, and sometimes behaving badly. Although his adult thinking became muddled, he never lost his childlike amazement at the little things we take for granted. Through it all, Dad's *core* remained the same, and I am so grateful that I went on this journey with him.

In Matthew chapter 18, verse 3, Jesus said, "Truly, I say to you, unless you turn and become like children, you will never enter the kingdom of Heaven." Surely Mil Hallenbeck, a child of God in every way, entered Heaven joyously singing *HALLELUJAH!*

The journey with dementia had ended at last.

The family at Dad's memorial service.
From left to right: Ginger, Kristen, John and Johnny McCulloch,
David, Steven, Lois, Bonnie, Bill and Gary Roesel

CHAPTER 17

REFLECTIONS

Being a nurse for over thirty years naturally helped me with the practical aspects of caring for my father. However, I learned so much more from this hands-on experience. Now that time has passed since his death, I can appreciate valuable lessons that enriched my life as a caregiver for an older person with dementia:

- ~ cherish the memories that do remain
- ~ capitalize on strengths
- ~ encourage activity and socialization
- ~ understand that a person with dementia is not crazy although the behavior may appear odd at times
- ~ focus on the positive; move ahead after setbacks
- ~ ask for relief from family
- ~ take the time to notice older people out in public; acknowledge their existence!
- ~ slow down to their pace and you will notice much more
- ~ sing! laugh! play! pray!
- ~ learn to be in the present and celebrate it!
- ~ know that love gets you through the hard times because it is stronger than fear

Parenting my father through his dementia opened my heart forever to a deeper compassion for the gift of life. Thank you, Dad, for this humbling experience and for an affirmation of what really matters. Helping you in your weakness made me a stronger person in the long run. It was an honor to know you in the sunset of your life.

CHAPTER 18

PAPA'S PRESENCE

In the months following my father's death, I returned to his house on a regular basis. There was much work to be done, sorting through his belongings and arranging for furniture to be delivered to various family members. I filled his garage with items that were picked up by a grateful pastor from Roselle for distribution to the poor. The piano went to a beloved musical friend of Dad's. Each grandchild had selected one of Papa's hats after his memorial service, and I gave away his ties to men who had a special connection in his life. I delivered the rest of his clothing to The Market Street Mission in Morristown.

I thought that I would feel sad going back into that silent house. As I worked, however, I felt incredibly peaceful. I was happy that his possessions were being spread out to so many different people, some of whom had never met Mil. The little solar-powered crystal in his window made rainbows which moved around the room where he had died. I felt comforted by this sign of Dad's presence and God's love. My niece Bonnie flew up from Tennessee and was a huge help in packing up her grandmother's china and other items. It felt good to laugh as we reminisced about Papa.

By now Bonnie was engaged to Dan Lawrence, and they were planning a wedding in July, 2003. Their local minister was to be away on vacation, so she was hoping that her grandfather's minister could marry them. Since Barrie Smith was retiring in June, he and Judy were free to come to Nashville for the marriage. We all felt that Papa's spirit helped make this re-connection possible. Barrie wore one of Mil's ties under his robe at the wedding and talked about him during the ceremony.

Within a few months, I was able to sell Dad's house privately. I know Mil's spirit will bless the new owners for years to come. As my son Johnny walked through the rooms one last time, happy childhood memories came flooding back. We all feel blessed to have had my father in our lives for such a long time.

In the fall of 2004, my daughter Kristen and I were busy with last-minute packing at her Kearny apartment in preparation for her move to California. As we began talking about Papa, we noticed a light in the bottom of a grocery bag across the room. We looked at each other and thought it was just a coincidence. I reached into the bag and found that a flashlight was on. After switching it off, I returned to my work. Soon the light went on again! We then went out for ice cream, excited about our cross-country drive, which would begin the next day on Papa's birthday. The light on her key chain went on and off a few times by itself. Was this another coincidence, or was he trying to get our attention? I believe we have much to learn about the spirit world.

Kristen and I felt Papa's presence all across the country as we laughed about all the silly things he did and said during his journey with dementia. We know now that we have a personal guardian angel watching over us, and as long as we keep his memory alive, his light will *never* go out!

SAMPLES OF MIL HALLENBECK'S WRITINGS

Long before his dementia set in, my father had a wonderful gift for writing. His use of the English language was unique, and I am delighted to share some of his talent with my readers. The earliest example is this thoughtful eulogy for his pet canary, penned in 1924 at the age of fourteen.

Our Canary

No life in that feathered body,
Nor song in that downy throat;
Cold death has come at last
And silenced your cheery note.

But eight short years you lived
(Or were they long to you?)
Eight years of caged living
(Pray – were we wrong to you?)

You sipped your water thru the day
And pecked away at seeds.
But never a moment could you chase
Those bugs on yonder weeds.

I'm told that this is for the best –
That you're far too weak to stray;
But would you be so awfully weak
Had you not been raised that way?

You're but the plaything of puzzled man
Who prates of liberty,
Yet holds you hostage caged for life
To ease his own captivity.

For three of your years you had a chum
Who sang in beauteous tone,
But he fell sick and died quite young
And left you to die alone.

You lived apart and died apart
From others of your kind;
A man would rather never be
Than face life so aligned.

But now in a heap on the floor of the cage
Rigid silence reigns;
But your spirit's winging with spirits of men
Alike released from pains.

For they say men go to heaven,
And they say it in so many words;
But surely if men merit heaven,
Why so do cage-weary birds?

Dad kept a diary from January to June of 1928, when he was a freshman at Dartmouth College. Besides recording events of the day, he jotted down thoughts or poetry each night. Here are some examples of his entries. I suspect they are original but have no way of knowing. They certainly reflect his love of the written word.

Music is a door through which a person may enter
realms of bewitching fantasy and enthralling beauty.

Perseverance is a quality we all admire;
yet so few of us can truthfully call that quality one of our characteristics.
We esteem the spider's persistence, the ant's repeated efforts;
yet how few of us emulate their examples.

Life's highway is a bleak one, yet dotted with cozy inns
and hospitable resting stations.
It is up to ourselves not to pass these by.
We cannot blame others if we plunge on all night or sleep in barren fields.

Why be pessimistic when there is so very much good in the world?
Our world has faults, but a perfect world would be unbearable.

Although we see, we are blind.
Because of our indifference, press of other affairs, or what not,
we fail to perceive the beauties of Nature,
except, perhaps, collectively.
And all this when the richest beauty in the world
lies in a tree, a flower, a bird.

The Rock of Ages is the rock of sages.

Lock before you sleep.

Only ignorance regards God and evolution enemies.

Enthusiasm is a great thing - indeed it is essential for complete
success. Yet we must not let ardor carry us away from the paths of
logic and common sense. Particularly dangerous is the ardor which
is aroused at the first mention of a project. If this is given full sway,
it soon burns itself out and leaves us weak and indifferent to the
continuation of the plan. This initial enthusiasm should be dammed
up and released little by little as occasion demands.

A loser usually finds an alibi;
It seems to be the nature of mankind;
But I oft have wondered why the alibi
so often shows ANOTHER man behind.

Talking about pets, my vote is for the dog. He is intelligent and a better
companion than any other animal.
I earnestly believe that at times a dog understands us better
than a human being does, because a dog's happiness
if not existence depends on our moods,
so he is therefore more observant of them.
A dog has as many advantages over a cat as he has over a tapeworm!

Fogs are caused by poor eyesight as well as by climatic conditions;
let us remember that when we apparently notice trouble.

A merry laugh is the richest possession we have.

To all who are troubled, I advise freedom from worry.
Yet I dread over-confidence to such an extent that I find relief in worry.
When I worry my mind is more at ease than one suspects, for I know
I cannot be disappointed - things cannot be worse than
I have imagined, whereas the chances are good of them being better.

When Spring her hand does first extend
And mighty Winter starts to bend
His haughty head, we feel new life
Go tingling through our veins. The knife
Of cold is gone from o'er our head,
And warmness, peace our lot instead.

A bud, so shy at first, grows fast
Until it forms a leaf at last.
A blade of grass peeps 'bove the soil
And shoves self up by strenuous toil.
And while we sit and humbly spy
Mosquitoes come and 'round us fly!

If a man has imagination, he has more pleasure than millionaires,
more enjoyment than the most renowned explorer, athlete, statesman.
He feasts himself on all their luxuries, imagined or real,
without any of their distressing drawbacks.
Imagination's one shortcoming is that it allows fear to creep in
where it does not belong.

Tidiness is not a fault, but is it the virtue people make it out to be
or is it just a practical aid?

The speck is worthless; yet with other specks it may be invaluable.

My favorite sample from my father's college diary expresses his
optimism:

Everything may not go smoothly all the time, but there are good things
in the past to look back upon - and what sweet food
reminiscences are! And the future is always bright,
if we will but assent to the hopeful mood, ever present for us to accept-
oil for the stormy seas of Life.

One of the many treasures that I discovered in Dad's attic was this
essay he wrote on August 3, 1938. Enjoy his clever wit as he writes
about, of all things, the art of chewing gum!

Gum chewing is now well established as an honorable
American custom. Although scolding school teachers and stern
bosses have for years done their utmost to stamp out the custom
as lacking in dignity, noisy and unworthy of a human being, they

have fought a losing battle against the combination of millions spent in advertising and the soothing capabilities of constant chewing. Teacher and boss each may still rule his tiny world, but outside of that they are hopelessly defeated. They may take comfort only in the knowledge that Americans chew only gum (and tobacco) and not the betel nut which leaves such juicy black stains on the teeth.

Although gum chewing is scarcely an art, there are several fairly well developed schools of mastication, and it is to these that I propose to give some slight attention. The manner of chewing adopted by a given person depends largely on the individual's temperament and upbringing, and also the particular mood he is in at the moment. There is a certain *savoir-faire* that distinguishes the gum chewing of Park Avenue Dorothea from that of 14th Street Rosie, and there is a world of difference between the casualness of certain inveterate chewers and the hasty amateurishness of the man who is trying to kill the odor of that forbidden cocktail before he gets home to wifie. Individual chewers ride the subways and walk the streets by the thousands, and it is only by examining the schools into which they fall that we may obtain any comprehensive knowledge of this Hogarthian habit.

There are two broad classifications: the Pugnacious or Active, and the Lackadaisical or Passive. Each contains several sub-classifications. Let us look first at the Pugnacious or Active chewers. These chewers as a general rule make chewing not only their own but their neighbor's business as well. Either the accompanying sound catches the neighbor's ear or the motion his eye, or both.

As our first sub-classification we have the Vindictive or Bone-Crusher chewer. This person chews as though he had a personal grudge against the gum. With swift, powerful strokes the luckless piece of gum is rapidly reduced to a pulp in the tyrant's mouth, and when the gum offers too little resistance by flattening out, the tongue curls it rapidly into shape for another crushing onslaught. This type occasionally errs by nipping the side of his cheek, but his gum bill is high as he is a constant chewer, and, due to his *modus operandi*, he gets very low mileage per stick of gum.

We also have the Staccato or Military type. The Military has nothing to do with a uniform, but it is used because of the regularity and precision of the strokes. In contrast to the Vindictive's comprehensive stroke which tries to squash the gum at one fell swoop, the Staccato's stroke, though firm, has more dignity, as if first trying to wear the gum down before administering the *coup de grace*. The regularity of the stroke is a marvel to behold, and hence the adoption of this school always denotes a professional. The ability to have the gum always in position and still not miss a stroke takes weeks of practice. Although a trifle nerve-racking to the on-looker, because of its increasing precision, this is really the least objectionable of the Pugnacious manners of mastication.

Thirdly, we have the Bovine or Rotary classification. Perilously close to a Lackadaisical manner, this is actually Pugnacious because of the enormous expenditure of effort involved. It consists of rolling the gum ponderously in a roughly circular orbit within the mouth. The gum is never sharply pierced, as it is in the Vindictive and Staccato manners, but it is kept in constant turmoil until it is finally worn to a frazzle. This type of chewing is ordinarily soundless, but it involves great physical exertion at all times, and even occasional contortions when the gum detours behind the lower lip. In fact, the Rotary chewers have been known to overturn a small rowboat in calm weather.

Lastly, we have the Talkative chewer. This type uses a very rapid stroke when in full swing, faster than the Staccato and lacking its regularity. The Talkative chewer seems to use gum as a tonic for the larynx, for once the gum is in the mouth, the stroke and conversation are begun immediately. Perhaps monologue is a better word, for a perfect stream of words well chopped up by the rapid strokes making an unintelligible jumble pours from the chewer's mouth. The stroke is generally up and down, but in the case of an individual who habitually speaks out of the side of his mouth, the stroke is northwest by southeast. This is the most exasperating type of chewer, for half the people in the vicinity know the individual is chewing gum but wonder why there is so much noise attached to it, and the other half think maybe he is trying to say something but can't tell what.

Now we come to the Lackadaisical or Passive classification. As the names imply, these chewers are generally of a retiring nature and do not obtrude the habit upon others. Some of them look as though they are chewing in their sleep, but they enjoy the sport in their own quiet way. They never bother the Pugnacious chewers, but often they seem to be suggesting by the daintiness of some of their strokes that there is a certain finesse to it after all.

First we have the Languid or Open-Mouthed type. This is frowned upon by real chewers as, in a sense, it is not chewing at all, for the upper teeth rarely come into contact with the gum. The gum rests upon the lower molars and the only action occurs when the under portion of the tongue flattens the gum out a bit. The mouth, of course, hangs open during the entire performance. This manner of chewing has a soothing effect on the individual which often induces sleep. However, no such escape can lure the onlooker, for when the gum is well flattened, and just before the mouth is temporarily shut to reform it into a ball, the chewer's gum usually protrudes slightly over the lower lip, and the chewer's neighbors are ever fearful that it won't be curled in time. Aside from causing this worry, the Languid chewer is not bothersome.

Secondly, there is the Pensive or Absentminded type. This stroke is similar to the Languid stroke except that the mouth is kept closed, and the chewer has a faraway look in the eye. The jaw movement is very slow. So gently is the gum treated that Vindictive chewers tear their hair at the sight of a Pensive chewer. The latter, surprising as it seems, has a high gum bill due to his proclivity for swallowing the gum while in a haze of forgetfulness. It is asserted that the stomach of a Pensive chewer is at best 45% coated with gum. The Pensive chewer is dull to watch and doesn't seem to derive much pleasure from the chewing, but it doubtless stimulates his daydreams.

Our next sub-classification is the Front Teeth or Rabbit chewer. Although a full-fledged chewer compared with the Lanquid type, the Rabbit chewer is more aptly a muncher. The stroke is fairly rapid, but short, lacking in force and done entirely in the front of the mouth as though the individual was breaking in a new set of teeth. This stroke is not calculated to do much damage to the gum, so that Rabbit munchers can, with favorable parking facilities, make one stick of gum last four or five days. Easy on the chewer and amusing to watch, this is a thoroughly delightful type.

Lastly, we have the Corkscrew or Creative type. Here the individual spares very little time chewing and most of the time modeling with his tongue. He grimaces as if in pain; he squints - every available facial expression is displayed by the Creative chewer at work. First the gum is in a perfectly round ball, then it is flattened into a narrow thin ribbon. Then it is split into two (and by experts four) parts, and they are separately molded to suit the person's whim. The Creative chewer gets very low mileage but sacrifices everything for form. This is an extremely satisfactory form of chewing for those who have a certain expertness with the tongue, and it is often resorted to by those for whom the glory of straightaway chewing has well nigh disappeared. Since some of the expressions are so frightening to behold, and the resulting creations are usually so well hidden from onlookers, it is a poor type to observe in action.

We have completed our analysis. Dozens of smaller classifications could be listed, but they can be grouped in the larger ones I have described. In general, Pugnacious chewers use heavier, more forceful strokes and their tolerance for non-chewers is surpassed only by their contempt for Lackadaisical chewers. The latter, with their daintier strokes, are complacent towards everyone, secure in their belief that their strokes approximate art.

In the 1950's Dad was on the planning board for the Cranford Swim Club. This was a major event in our town, and the meetings held many challenges. Leave it to my father to write a poem about the experience! Note: Brown refers to a councilman at the time.

"There's many a slip 'twixt the cup and and the lip,"
The ancient poet said.
"The understatement of all time,"
Say we with nodding head.

Here at last in crystal clearness,
Culminating fondest dreams,
Lies this mass of azure wetness,
Cooler even than it seems.

Ah, what a winding road we wend
On the way to the witching water,
A road through groves more Brown than green
And township hearings not quite serene,
With sessions long but tempers shorter.

Suits on file and suits a-threatening
Keep us plenty busy
Round and round about we go,
Is everybody dizzy?

The arguments of lawyers
May benefit men and women,
But they simply won't hold water
That our membership can swim in.

Scarcely the type of structure
To accommodate our mermaids and mermen
Is the spacious county courthouse
With its jail for in stir-men.

Then we choose the current site -
And lo! - a new instigator -
Pencil and paper, petitions to write
Oh, Lord! Not another litigator!

Pawnee, Shawnee, Chippewa brave
Donned warpaint and feather;
But the tom-toms were snuffed and peacepipe puffed
When both sides got together.

Through days and days of all delays
Our optimism rampant,
We had no pool but still kept cool;
Our spirits were undampant.

Now at last we're on the ball
And things are far from grim
As we hear that long-awaited call -
Everybody swim!

My father wrote this lovely romantic poem for my mother on their
first wedding anniversary in 1940. I believe that I have saved the best
for last.

Would that I the stars could pluck
From out of cosmic space,
And pick the ageless, yellow moon
From its accustomed place:
I'd give into my sweetheart's care
These diamonds of the skies,
And bid her wear them in her hair
To match the sparkle in her eyes.

Would that I a mansion owned
Upon a vast estate,
Filled with graceful furnishings,
Bright and up-to-date;
The mansion's door I'd fling so wide
To greet my sweetheart-wife,
For she of all must there abide
To bring it mirthful life.

Would that I a poet were,
To sing in lyric measure,
To write in winged words just how
Her smile fills me with pleasure,
To tell to all the distant earth
How daily grows my love
For her whose winsome charm is worth
To me more than all else above.

A million courses I could pursue
My sweet one's heart and hand to woo;
But they all call for genius or money,
So, lacking these.....a flower, Honey.

NOTES

CHAPTERS 1 AND 7

Information on the signs and symptoms of dementia and Alzheimer's disease is based on *Recognition and Initial Assessment of Alzheimer's Disease and Related Dementias: Clinical Practice Guideline* No. 19; The Agency for Health Care Policy and Research (AHCPR); U. S. Department of Health and Human Services, September 1996.

CHAPTER 3

Facts regarding college admission and the New England flood in 1927 were taken from the newsletter *The Dartmouth,* published in Hanover, NH, June 9, 1996.

CHAPTER 5

The mini-mental exam I gave my father is from Folstein, M.E. and Folstein, S.E. *Mini-mental state: A practical method for grading the cognitive state of patients for the clinician.* Journal of Psychiatric Research 12:189-198, 1975.

CHAPTER 7

Anosmia (definition): Taber's cyclopedic medical dictionary, edition 15, 1985. F. A. Davis Co. p. 99

Sniff Test: *Johns Hopkins White Papers on Memory 2008;* published by Johns Hopkins Medicine, Baltimore. MD.

Facts about 1910 were taken from a Hallmark greeting card entitled: *1910 Was a wonderful year...*

Hospice information is taken from the website www.hospicenet.org

CHAPTER 8

Chutes and Ladders, Candy Land, and Scrabble are all Milton Bradley games

Reminiscence Therapy for Dementia is from an abstract by Woods, Spector, Jones, Orrell, and Davies from The Cochrane Library, Issue 2, 2005. Chichester, UK: John Wiley & sons, Ltd.

Song Titles: *Ein Prosit* is a traditional German drinking song; unknown composer

Jesus Loves Me is a children's hymn; unknown composer

Row Row Row Your Boat and *Farmer in the Dell* are traditional childrens' songs; unknown composers

Good Night, Irene; 1933; Ledbetter-Lomax

Shave and a Hair Cut, Two Bits! is a traditional American song; unknown composer

Swanee River (Old Folks at Home) is by Foster; year
unknown
Polly Wolly Doodle; 1883; traditional black American
minstrel song
I've Been Workin' on the Railroad; 1880; traditional
American folksong

CHAPTER 12

Michael Hingson is now the National Public Affairs and Donor Relations
Director for Guide Dogs for the Blind. You can learn more about him
and Roselle on his website www.guidedogs.com/bios-hingson.html

CHAPTER 14

Sundowning or sundowner's syndrome (definition): Fundamentals of
Nursing by Kozier, Erb, Blais, and Wilkinson, fifth edition, p. 719.
Menlo Park, CA: Addison Wesley Longman, Inc. 1998.

Hallelujah! I'm a Bum: written by Harry McClintock as a Union song
for the IWW and a musical movie starring Al Jolson in 1933. Website
sources:
www.smithsonianmag.si.edu/smithsonian/issues98/aug98/hobo.html
http://www/dinesp.fsnet.co.uk/hallel.html

A FEW NOTES ABOUT ALZHEIMER'S DISEASE

DAVID J. ROESEL MD, MPH

Dr. David Roesel, Grandson

This book tells the story of how my grandfather became more and more disconnected from his own past, his memories, and the world around him, until little was left but the beauty of his spirit. It is a tale of discovery, as my aunt faced challenges, frustrations, and joys while caring for him along this journey. Although my grandfather's story is a personal one, the type of cognitive deterioration from which he suffered is one that affects millions of Americans and their loved ones.

The medical term for my grandfather's illness is Alzheimer's disease, which is the most common form of dementia affecting the elderly. Over 4.5 million Americans presently suffer from this disease, and this number is expected to triple by 2050. Alzheimer's disease has claimed the lives of several prominent figures, including Ronald Reagan and Rita

Hayworth, and it is currently the fourth leading cause of death for those over 65. Alzheimer's affects one out of four nursing home residents, and it carries an estimated societal cost of 100 billion dollars per year. The emotional cost to families and loved ones is immeasurable.

Alzheimer's disease is different from the normal slowing of intellectual functioning that can occur as people age. In Alzheimer's, the mental deterioration begins slowly but progresses persistently to the point of profound incapacity and eventual death. The disease is caused by the abnormal accumulation of certain types of proteins within the brain, identified on autopsy as *plaques and tangles.* In the early stages, common features are impairment of short-term memory, difficulties with language, and trouble with calculations, planning, organization, and judgment. Household finances may fall into disarray, shopping and meal planning may become a challenge, and the person may fall prey to unscrupulous solicitors. Family members may notice the affected relative getting lost, struggling to find things, or having difficulties with concentration and attention. More childlike behaviors and traits may begin to surface, and the person may have difficulties controlling their emotions. In the earlier stages of Alzheimer's, personality, more remote memories, and social graces are relatively well-preserved, and the affected person can often hide his or her impairments. Frequently, it is often not until a crisis occurs that the severity of the problem finally comes to light.

As Alzheimer's disease progresses, the memory losses become more and more profound, and the world can seem to the patient an increasingly alien and frightening place. The person loses the ability to recognize familiar people and places and becomes easily confused and disoriented. Speaking and understanding others becomes more difficult, and dealing with the simple tasks of daily life, such as dressing, bathing, and eating becomes a struggle. Psychiatric symptoms, such as depression, irritability, apathy, paranoia or delusions may develop. Appearance and hygiene become neglected, and behavior becomes more uninhibited. There is often increasing agitation, particularly at night, wandering, sleep disturbance, socially inappropriate behaviors, emotional outbursts, and even aggression. The affected person may even become convinced that a caregiver has been replaced by an imposter. These changes in behavior are often extremely distressing to loved ones, and caregivers can find themselves emotionally exhausted.

In the final stages of Alzheimer's, the person can become physically more rigid and slow and will ultimately become confined to bed. By this stage, they are often severely withdrawn and unable to communicate. Bladder and bowel incontinence develops, and feeding becomes a challenge. The person becomes completely dependent on others for care. Death generally occurs within ten years after diagnosis.

It is not entirely clear why some people develop Alzheimer's disease and others do not, but a number of predisposing factors have been identified. Advanced age is the biggest risk factor: the chance of having the disease is only 5 percent at age 70, but it jumps to 50 percent by age 90. There is also a genetic predisposition: Alzheimer's is three to four times more likely in someone with an affected parent or sibling, and most people with the genetic defect causing Down's syndrome develop Alzheimer's by age 40. Women, particularly those who take hormones after the age of 65, seem to have a greater risk, as do people with diabetes, high blood pressure, and high cholesterol. Exposures to various toxins have been implicated in disease development, but research has yet to turn up anything conclusive. Aluminum cookware, for example, was once suspected of being a cause, but years of research have failed to find any link between aluminum exposure and Alzheimer's disease.

Once dementia is suspected in a loved one, it is important to seek medical advice. Nearly half of all cases of dementia are caused by conditions other than Alzheimer's disease, and many of these conditions can improve with treatment. For example, mental functioning can be impaired by alcohol use, medication side-effects, depression, thyroid disorders, vitamin deficiencies, and certain types of infections. Multiple small strokes, bleeding around the brain, and brain tumors can also cause dementia. A medical evaluation can help to confirm the diagnosis of dementia through a detailed medical history (including talking to family members), physical exam, and neurological and cognitive testing. The doctor should be told of all medications, including over-the-counter drugs and dietary supplements, to ensure that none of these are contributing to symptoms. Although there is no specific test which can diagnose Alzheimer's disease (which can only be confirmed by brain biopsy during autopsy), laboratory tests and diagnostic imaging are frequently performed to rule-out other common or treatable causes of dementia. A typical work-up will include screening for infection, thyroid imbalance, electrolyte abnormalities, syphilis, vitamin B12 deficiency, along with brain imaging with CT or MRI scanning.

There is currently no cure for Alzheimer's disease. Nothing has yet been found which can reverse or stop the progressive destruction of brain cells caused by this illness. There are, however, a few drugs licensed for use in Alzheimer's, and they can provide some limited improvements in mental functioning and behavioral symptoms. Three of these medications, *Aricept* (donepezil), *Razadyne* (galantamine), and *Exelon* (rivastigmine), work by increasing brain levels of acetylcholine, a chemical associated with learning and memory which is depleted in the brains of Alzheimer's patients. The most common side effects are nausea, vomiting, and diarrhea, which can be lessened if the pills are taken with meals. All three of these drugs appear to have similar efficacy and cost, although they differ somewhat in dosing schedules and side-effect profiles. *Namenda* (memantine) is a newer Alzheimer's drug which works by a different mechanism. It is generally well-tolerated and can be used in combination with one of the medications above to further reduce symptoms in patients with moderate to severe dementia. Newer generation antipsychotic drugs such as *Risperdal* (risperidone) and *Zyprexa* (olanzapine) are often used to help calm agitated patients with dementia, although the FDA has warned that such use carries an increased risk of mortality. There has also been interest in treating or preventing Alzheimer's with antioxidants like vitamin E, or with herbal supplements such as Ginkgo biloba, omega-3 fatty acids, or huperzine A, but there is currently insufficient data to recommend the use of these agents. It is worth remembering that aggressive medical treatment does not improve survival in Alzheimer's disease and can increase patient discomfort.

A number of non-pharmacologic measures can be helpful in caring for people with Alzheimer's. It is important to maintain mental stimulation, physical activity, social interaction, and proper nutrition. Sedating medications such as Benadryl should be avoided. Safety becomes a big concern: car keys may need to be removed, and some form of identification should be provided in case the person becomes lost. The home may need to be modified to ensure good lighting, lack of clutter, and removal or unplugging of dangerous appliances. Written reminders placed around the house can be helpful. Consistent daily routines and rituals are encouraged. The goal is to provide a safe, sheltered, predictable and loving environment in which the person's dignity and autonomy are respected as much as possible. As the disease progresses, the responsibilities of the caregiver will inevitably increase, and the physical and emotional toll can become harder to bear. Reaching out to others for assistance is vital to prevent caregiver-burnout. Luckily, there are a number of good resources for families and patients to learn more about the disease and to turn for help. Here is a partial listing:

Alzheimer's Disease Education and Referral Center (ADEAR)
P.O. Box 8250
Silver Spring, MD 20907-8250
adear@nia.nih.gov
http://www.alzheimers.nia.nih.gov
Tel: 301-495-3311 800-438-4380
Fax: 301-495-3334

National Institute of Mental Health (NIMH)
National Institutes of Health, DHHS
6001 Executive Blvd. Rm. 8184, MSC 9663
Bethesda, MD 20892-9663
nimhinfo@nih.gov
http://www.nimh.nih.gov
Tel: 301-443-4513/866-615-NIMH (-6464) 301-443-8431 (TTY)
Fax: 301-443-4279

Alzheimer's Association
225 North Michigan Avenue
17th Floor
Chicago, IL 60601-7633
info@alz.org
http://www.alz.org
Tel: 312-335-8700 800-272-3900
Fax: 312-335-1110

Alzheimer's Foundation of America
322 Eighth Avenue
6th Floor
New York, NY 10001
info@alzfdn.org
http://www.alzfdn.org
Tel: 866-AFA-8484 (232-8484)
Fax: 646-638-1546

Family Caregiver Alliance/National Center on Caregiving
180 Montgomery Street
Suite 1100
San Francisco, CA 94104
info@caregiver.org
http://www.caregiver.org
Tel: 415-434-3388 800-445-8106
Fax: 415-434-3508

National Family Caregivers Association
10400 Connecticut Avenue
Suite 500
Kensington, MD 20895-3944
info@thefamilycaregiver.org
http://www.thefamilycaregiver.org
Tel: 301-942-6430 800-896-3650
Fax: 301-942-2302

Well Spouse Association
63 West Main Street
Suite H
Freehold, NJ 07728
info@wellspouse.org
http://www.wellspouse.org
Tel: 800-838-0879 732-577-8899
Fax: 732-577-8644

National Respite Network and Resource Center
800 Eastowne Drive
Suite 105
Chapel Hill, NC 27514
http://www.archrespite.org
Tel: 919-490-5577 x222
Fax: 919-490-4905

American Health Assistance Foundation
22512 Gateway Center Drive
Clarksburg, MD 20871
info@ahaf.org
http://www.ahaf.org
Tel: 301-948-3244 800-437-AHAF (2423)
Fax: 301-258-9454

National Hospice and Palliative Care Organization/National Hospice Foundation
1700 Diagonal Road
Suite 625
Alexandria, VA 22314
nhpco_info@nhpco.org
http://www.nhpco.org
Tel: 703-837-1500 Helpline: 800-658-8898
Fax: 703-837-1233

Alzheimer's Drug Discovery Foundation
1414 Avenue of the Americas
Suite 1502
New York, NY 10019
hfillit@alzdiscovery.org
http://www.alzdiscovery.org
Tel: 212-935-2402
Fax: 212-935-2408

John Douglas French Alzheimer's Foundation
11620 Wilshire Blvd.
Suite 270
Los Angeles, CA 90025
jdfaf@earthlink.net
http://www.jdfaf.org
Tel: 310-445-4650 800-477-2243
Fax: 310-479-0516

SOURCES

Abraham, I.L. Dementia and Alzheimer's Disease: A Practical
    Orientation. *Nursing Clinics of North America,* 2006; 41: 19-
    127.

Bird, T.D. and Miller, B.L. Alzheimer's Disease and Other
    Dementias. *Harrison's Principals of Internal Medicine, 16th ed.*
    McGraw Hill (NY), 2005; 2393-2406.

Desai, A.K. and Grossberg, G.T. Diagnosis and Treatment of
    Alzheimer's Disease. *Neurology,* 2005 June; 64 (Supplement
    3): S34-39.

Drugs for Cognitive Loss and Dementia. Treatment Guidelines from
    the Medical Letter, 2007; 5(54): 9-14.

Hitzeman, N. Cholinesterase inhibitors for Alzheimer's Disease.
    American Family Physician, 2006 Sept 1. 74(5): 747-9.

Yaari, R. and Corey-Bloom, J. Alzheimer's Disease. *Seminars in
    Neurology,* 2007; 27: 32-41.

Made in the USA
Lexington, KY
29 December 2012